A STUDY OF TEN POINTS IN EVIDENCE
FOR DIVINE AUTHORITY

THE
SUPERNATURAL ORIGIN
OF THE BIBLE

by **KENNETH JAMES NETTLES, Th.D.**
Chaplain (First Lieutenant), U.S.A.F.

Foreword by Eugene T. Pratt

An Exposition–Testament Book

EXPOSITION PRESS NEW YORK

Exposition Press Inc., 386 Fourth Avenue, New York 16, N.Y.

FIRST EDITION

To those able teachers who have been unashamed
to express confidence in the Bible
as God's standard for man's religious life

FOREWORD

Belief in the trustworthiness of the Bible as the inspired word of God is fundamental to the Christian faith. An intelligent and healthy faith always demands satisfactory evidence for its support.

This volume is the result of the author's quest to find adequate evidence to support his belief in the Bible. The quest has been made at the cost of diligent research in many fields, such as ancient history, Biblical archaeology, comparative religion, noncanonical Jewish writings, and the original texts of the Scriptures. Only the best in scholarship, united with a genuine faith, could have produced a volume such as this.

Careful students will gratefully accept this well-written and well-documented book. The evidence is weighed and presented with effectiveness. Problems related to the Christian faith are never settled until one settles them for himself, with divine help. But here is a volume that will help each of us settle once and for all our faith in the Scriptures.

Perhaps many who will be helped by these pages will never have the opportunity to know the author personally. His scholastic training, his hunger for accuracy, his humble faith, his experience as pastor and chaplain in the United States Air Force, qualify him to aid us in the quest that we, too, would make in an effort to strengthen our faith.

Eugene T. Pratt, *Pastor*
Westview Baptist Church

Belleville, Illinois

CONTENTS

SYNOPSIS:

The Ten Points in Evidence for the Supernatural Origin of the Bible

I. The Bible is intuitively recognized as the word of God. If one will trust the welfare of his person to the message of the Bible, turn loose his inhibitions and let the Book speak, he will find that it is the communication of God to his soul.

II. The many various writings, produced through men of diverse personalities over a period of fifteen centuries, continually and consistently claim to be of supernatural origin. This fact is unique among religious writings.

III. There is a humanly inexplicable unity and direction in the movement of thought in the many diverse Scriptures.

IV. The Bible has shown an amazing historical accuracy in the face of ruthless criticism.

V. The Bible offers the only satisfactory explanation of origins.

VI. The Bible speaks with accuracy concerning scientific facts known to man only in recent times.

VII. The Bible contains a number of predictions which have been fulfilled in ways that preclude human fore-knowledge.

VIII. The Hebrew-Christian Scriptures consistently place full blame upon humanity for failure to produce a righteous society on earth. We would not expect human nature to claim failure for itself. All other philosophies tend to excuse man.

IX. The Bible offers the only satisfactory solution to the problem of sin.

X. The Bible produces miraculous improvements in the lives of fallen men.

INTRODUCTION

WHEN THE AUTHOR was a lad in college, he one day asked himself the question, "All the years of my remembrance I have believed the Bible to be the authoritative Word of God; but what evidence is there to substantiate this belief?" He began to ask his fellow students the same question, and hinted to some of his professors the problem that disturbed his rest; but none of them gave him a satisfactory answer. Then, to make matters worse, one of the professors began to suggest that perhaps his belief in the authority of the Bible was misguided. Was the very standard by which he felt he had come to know God untrustworthy? Was the Bible only a record of the ethical struggle of the Jews and Christians, like any other of the world's great religious writings, helpful in the development of a man's religious nature but not the definite disclosure of God's will for man?

Then one day this professor told the young student that a considerable number of professors in our seminaries held the evolutionary view. This the student could hardly believe; but he found it to be true. "The Bible is not the authority," he was told; "the authority is personal experience." When the student found that many of his fellow theological students were accepting this view, he did some serious soul-searching. If so many brilliant and able minds had rejected the tradition of the authority of the Bible, the reasons must be good. Here are some statements characteristic of the attitudes he discovered against the authority of the Bible:

The view taken in this book is that the supernatural can have a profitable place in today's and tomorrow's religion only as the value seen in it is the value of poetry and folklore. Thus understood, we can appreciate and use the supernatural. But supernaturalism, with its continued fostering of attempts in one way or another to draw unique and ultimate truth from folklore, is a thing we should abandon.[1]

It [the oldest element of the Hexateuch] was the first sustained history to be written anywhere. . . . The writer . . . wrote his book about 850 B.C. in the Southern Kingdom of Judah.[2]

Arnold Toynbee speaks of "the myth of the Expulsion from Eden and . . . the myth of the Exodus from Egypt"[3] and of the "Syriac myth of Moses' solitary ascent of Mount Sinai."[4] Edmund Soper decries the fact that "having overturned the authority of the visible Church, it [the Reformation] set up another authority in its place, that of the infallible Bible."[5]

. . . Nahum is on a much lower spiritual level than Amos, and the Book of Revelation in the New Testament is morally inferior to the writings of the Great Isaiah in the Old Testament.[6]

By the showing of the Bible itself (see Ex. 12:40) there is a gap of 430 years, during which the Hebrews were in Egypt and nothing whatever is recorded. From the Exodus to the writing down of the J document (see INTRODUCTION TO THE PENTATEUCH) another 400 years or so passed. What probability is there that genuine traditions were transmitted over so long a period? We conclude that what happened before the Exodus is pre-history, in the sense of being based on oral tradition of things that had been imprinted on the folk memory.[7]

The student decided to give the matter his utmost attention. The resulting study is a matter that began in college, continued through attendance at two seminaries and on into the pastorate and the chaplaincy. Always there has been the tension between the two attitudes toward the Bible. Those who reject the authority of the Bible, whether they prefer that of the ecclesiastical organization, or of personal experi-

---

1. Frank and Mildred Eakin, *Let's Think About Our Religion*, p. 133.
2. Edgar Goodspeed, *The Story of the Old Testament*, p. 107.
3. *A Study of History*, p. 99.
4. *Ibid.*, p. 217.
5. *The Religions of Mankind*, p. 331.
6. H. E. Fosdick, *A Guide to the Understanding of the Bible*, p. xiii.
7. W. K. L. Clarke, *Concise Bible Commentary*, p. 10.

ence, or of some other book, all have much in common in
their attitude toward the Bible.

Although I have sat at the feet of many splendid conservative theological teachers, in the course of my formal
education, the bulk of the suggested material discussing the
inspiration of the Scriptures and related themes, such as the
Virgin Birth of Jesus, his substitutionary atonement, and his
bodily return, was in the theologically liberal vein. I began
to feel that if competent scholars had little to say on the
other side, it must be because there was nothing substantial
to be said. It was in such a distracted state of mind that I
found and read *The Five Books of Moses,* by Oswald T.
Allis, *Fellowship in the Life Eternal,* by G. G. Findlay, *The
Gospel According to St. John,* by W. B. Westcott, and a few
others, with their firm belief in the elemental truths which
come from an humble acceptance of the genuineness of the
Bible. It was with deep emotion that I studied their reasonable answers to the attacks made upon the conservative
viewpoint. Then I asked, "Why must the arguments on one
side of so great an issue come almost incidentally or accidentally to the attention of the student who is trying to
come to a knowledge of the truth about it?" I eventually
concluded that there are two reasons: (1) the advocates of
the liberal viewpoint, who are in the large majority among
religious educators, are lax in pointing out to their students
the weighty arguments of strong conservative scholars, and
(2) conservative people have been too timid in contending
for their faith before the bar of intellectual opinion. We have
long felt that our gospel is not concerned with intellectual-
ism, and therefore we have not argued with the intellectuals
However, we forget that we are sending our youth to sit
at the feet of the intellectuals to have their doctrinal outlook
molded. While stoutly advocating education of the highest
kind, we ignore the fact that, by and large, we have surrendered that education, by default, to the theologically
liberal viewpoint. No wonder Christianity, as a whole, is
tending to become non-Biblical or even anti-Biblical. Bib-

lical Christians should increasingly place before the developing minds of our youth strong reading matter in support of the conservative faith.

The author frankly confesses that he has not been coldly objective throughout the course of this study. As a matter of fact, from the beginning he has had a feeling that the Bible is true and is God's objective standard for human redemption and behavior, because the most valued experience of his life came about on the basis of that attitude toward the Bible message—the experience of choosing Jesus Christ as his personal Lord and Saviour. It is true that this is subjective, and cannot of itself be the principal evidence in the courts of academic logic. But it is not contrary to logic. Indeed, some of the most important scientific discoveries of all time have been made because someone had an intuition that a certain idea was true in the natural world and set about to prove it. Marconi felt that messages could be sent long distances through the air without the use of wires; and at length he proved it. Goodyear had an intuition that crude rubber could be treated in such a way as to make it resilient for a thousand personal and industrial uses. After many failures his intuition was finally supported when he accidentally spilled some crude rubber on a hot stove. A lawyer may take a case that seems to have all the evidence against it, and yet find evidence to vindicate his client. In much the same way, the author has felt that the idea is true that the Bible is the standard of God for men, and that if it is true, there must be plenty of evidence for it. That evidence has not been found lacking.

The one thing in common about all the criticisms brought against the authority of the Bible is that they cannot stand the test of intensive criticism of themselves. The Bible is an ancient book written in languages we do not speak today. Much of the history of those times is shrouded in darkness. The outstanding weakness of the adverse critics is that they are too hasty in assuming a Biblical error. Scores of times the objections have melted away as more information on

the subject was discovered. This is the phenomenon that
has impressed the author most. It has so often occurred in
his experience as to become to him almost a law of Biblical
study, that if enough critical investigation is applied to the
adverse criticism, it will in time yield.

The author has found ten evidences for the supernatural
origin of the Bible, one of them highly subjective and the
others highly objective. No doubt there are others; but these
are presented in the hope that some who are considering
discarding the age-old belief in the Bible as the Word of
God may think again before they throw away the most
precious part of their heritage.

Perhaps a word should be said about textual criticism,
since the authority of the Bible is often questioned on the
grounds of variations in the many manuscripts. The answer
is simple. God at various times and in various manners
supernaturally communicated his will to his servants. He
trusted those who love him to preserve faithfully, by human
means, the precious messages superhumanly given. His confidence was not misfounded. One of the leading authorities
in the field of textual criticism concludes that there is less
than a thousandth of the New Testament text about which
there is any real question.[8] The outstanding thing is not
that there are so many variations, but that there are so few.
The recent discovery of the Dead Sea scrolls has under-
scored the carefulness with which the scribes transmitted
the Scriptures. The text of Isaiah is essentially the same as
we have it two thousand years later. There is not enough
difference in the manscripts of the Bible to form any prominent part in a discussion as to its total meaning.

A knowledge of the process of canonization of the writings that now constitute our Bible will help one to see the
unusual care which the Jews and early Christians took to
insure that the divine writings were kept distinct from those

---

8. A. T. Robertson, *An Introduction to the Textual Criticism of the
New Testament*, p. 22.

of human inspiration. That the Jews rejected from the canon *Bel and the Dragon, The Wisdom of Sirach, Judith, The Wisdom of Solomon, Tobit* and other similar interesting books, and that the Christians rejected *The Gospel of Peter, The Protevangelium of James, The Passing of Mary, The Acts of John* and other like writings about Christian subjects may in itself be viewed as an evidence for the supernatural preservation of the Bible. However, since some of the sacred scriptures of other religions went through somewhat similar processes in their canonization, this author prefers to regard the process of Bible canonization as a result generally of God's reliance upon human recognition of the divine word as opposed to the human. The very presence of a genuine message from God among men would serve to sharpen their perceptive powers. The fact that the Jews and early Christians did indeed have a genuine supernatural revelation makes the canonization process in other religions a mere shadow of the real separating process that went on with respect to the Bible.

Webster's definition of the word "supernatural" is the one intended in the title and throughout the text of this book: "Of, or proceeding from, an order of existence beyond nature, or the visible and observable universe." [9]

---

9. *Webster's Collegiate Dictionary,* Fifth Edition.

THE

SUPERNATURAL ORIGIN

OF

THE BIBLE

CHAPTER I ❧ *The Bible is intuitively recognized as the word of God. If one will trust the welfare of his person to the message of the Bible, turn loose his inhibitions and let the Book speak, he will find that it is the communication of God to his soul.*

INTUITIVE RECOGNITION

How CAN IT be proved that a sunset or a masterpiece of art is beautiful? When one sees a healthy, well-developed rose, he does not go through a process of logic to arrive at the conclusion that here is an altogether lovely sight. In the same way, the Bible is spontaneously recognized as divine truth wherever it is presented to people who have not had occasion to be influenced against it.

A missionary for twenty years, during which time he saw the Bible's reception by many different peoples, Arthur M. Chirgwin, Research Secretary of the United Bible Societies, has made a study in which he cites numbers of instances where unprejudiced peoples have recognized the Bible to be the divine standard. He points out that man has a heart that is sick, and yearning for the key to soul satisfaction in a world that is full of suffering and injustice. When men are confronted with the Bible message, there usually springs up within them the recognition that here is the long-sought-after solution.

There is, for example, the story of Tommer, an educated Mongolian who found himself under the spell of the very words that made a new man of Ishii. Tommer was by nature hard and unyielding, and when he agreed in 1943 to help two missionaries who were revising the Mongolian New Testament, he did so with a completely closed mind. He would elucidate and mark down the words he thought ought to be changed. But if any attempt was made to explain some Bible truth to him a stern look came over his face and he became as hard and cold as steel. In this way the Gospels of Matthew, Mark and Luke were gone through until the thirty-fourth verse of the twenty-third chapter of St. Luke was reached: "Jesus said, 'Father, forgive them, for they know not what they do.'" Suddenly Tommer seemed to forget all about the two missionaries and, reading the verse over and over again, he burst into tears and going down on his knees said, "O Lord, I see it now; it was all for me." From that day he was a changed man and became a lover of the Bible and one whose witness was moving to hear.[1]

He multiplies incidents such as this:

A better-known example of conversion following upon the reading of the Bible is that of the proud Confucian scholar of the old school, destined to become one of the evangelists of Central China and known to the world as Pastor Hsi. A man of culture and education, Hsi tended to keep himself aloof. Preaching left him unmoved. Even the personal friendship of the saintly David Hill was not enough to bring him to the point of decision. It was a copy of the Chinese New Testament, left deliberately on his study table, that succeeded where other means failed. He picked it up and with some hesitation opened it and began to read. As he read on and on, and especially as he neared the end of the Gospel narrative, a curtain seemed to be lifted. He seemed to see the Lord and hear His Word. That decided him. He knelt down there and then and acknowledged Christ as his Saviour and Lord. When he stood up again it was to start on a course from which he never turned back.[2]

Then there is the case of a man who had received no Christian influence at all, except a portion of the New Testament:

The case of John Subhan, now a Bishop of the Methodist Church in North India, is even more remarkable, not only because he was a loyal Moslem, but also because he was a strict member of the Sufi sect. As a boy he attended a Moslem school, studied the Koran under the direction of the mullah, and lived in an

1. A. M. Chirgwin, *The Bible in World Evangelism*, pp. 66–67.
2. *Ibid.*, p. 68.

entirely Moslem setting. He had no associations of any kind
with Christian people or Christian institutions. To the best of
his knowledge he had never met either a missionary or an Indian
pastor. He had never heard a Christian address and had certainly
never listened to a Christian sermon. But he had read a Gospel!
Just one! "It was sufficient," he said. "It convinced me and I
decided to become a Christian." There was apparently no other
agency at work except the single Gospel. It is that simple fact, or
something like it, that stands out in all these cases.[3]

Again, he tells of an ex-convict, who

. . . was in fact on his way to join his old gang with a view to
another burglary when he picked a man's pocket in Fifth Avenue,
New York, and slipping into Central Park to see what he had
acquired, found himself in possession of a New Testament. Having time to spare before joining his comrades, he sat down and
began to read. Soon he was deep in the book, and he read to
such effect that a few hours later he went to his comrades and
told them bluntly what he had been doing, and broke with them
for good.[4]

Here we see that the gangster found the Bible to be the
sufficient answer to his hidden yearning for truth and right.
Another case shows how the Bible gave a man a solution
to his problem that he knew to be divine, for he had never
conceived it or heard of it before:

"I had made up my mind to kill him," he confessed recently to
a Bible society colporteur. "I hated him so much that I plotted
revenge, even to the point of murder. Then one day I ran into
you and you induced me to buy a copy of St. Matthew. I only
bought it to please you. I never intended to read it. But as I
was going to bed that night the book fell out of my pocket and
I picked it up and started to read. When I reached the place
where it says, 'Ye have heard that it was said by them of old
time, Thou shalt not kill. . . . But I say unto you that whosoever
is angry with his brother without a cause shall be in danger of
judgment,' I remembered the hatred I was nourishing against

---

3. *Ibid.*, p. 70.
4. *Ibid.*, p. 71.

my enemy. As I read on my uneasiness grew until I reached the words, 'Come unto me all ye who labour and are heavy laden, and I will give you rest. Take my yoke upon you, and learn of me; for I am meek and lowly in heart; and ye shall find rest unto your souls.' Then I was compelled to cry: 'God be merciful to me a sinner.' Joy and peace filled my heart and my hatred disappeared. Since then I have been a new man and my chief delight is to read God's Word." [5]

The story of the Karens of Burma will be recalled. Adoniram Judson had labored many years without success in Burma when one day he happened to converse with some strange mountain people. His Bible came to their attention and deeply interested them because it was black. "We have a tradition," said they, "that a white brother would come with a black book from God to tell us the way of salvation." The Karens learned the message of the book and found it to fulfill ther highest expectations. From this striking circumstance many thousands of them were converted and baptized.

Many times, on the mission field, recognition comes without any prior preparation other than the longing of the human heart for just such a message. "No one can travel much in Latin America without coming upon church after church that had its origin in some group that first met for Bible reading." [6]

Towards the end of 1936 a rumour went round amongst the Protestants in Lima that in an up-country area four groups of people were meeting regularly for Bible study, but had only one Bible between them! A visit was arranged, and it was discovered that these four groups had come into being through reading a copy of a Bible which had been found in an old trunk. How it got there no one knew. All that was known was that when it was found it was handed round and read by one person after another, and in time four groups began to meet to study it in turn. These four groups were afterwards formed into four evangelical congre-

---

5. *Ibid.*, pp. 71–72.
6. *Ibid.*, p. 81.

gations, and still later they became the nucleus of a properly constituted Presbytery. Many of the churches of Peru were, like this one, little more than Bible-reading groups in the first instance.[7]

The first Baptist church to be organized in the far interior of Brazil came about in a similar manner.

In the far interior, where no preacher had ever been, a merchant got hold of a Bible. He began to read it. Then he told his neighbors about it—"This wonderful book of God," as they called it. Crowds began to gather every Sunday for the reading of the Word and prayer. Numbers were converted and even before they had heard of the missionaries. When word reached them of the Baptists at Bahia, they begged Dr. Taylor to come and baptize them. The result was a Baptist church, the first in the far interior.[8]

In a land that has been long dominated by a religious system which discourages Bible reading, a Catholic Bible itself has served the purpose of changing a large part of an interior village over to the evangelical faith. A Catholic gentleman had sent a letter to the colporteur asking for a Catholic Bible, which the latter after some difficulty obtained for him. The man, having been told of the harm of the Protestant Bible, had refused any but the "approved" Bible. Within three months the colporteur received a letter asking for "prayer for my conversion," which soon came about. The colporteur writes:

Since then I have made a journey to his town, and found that the Pope's Bible has done wonders indeed. . . . Not only Senhor Luiz himself, but many neighbors and friends had also taken the same step. . . . To my astonishment I found a fine Gospel Mission Hall, one of the best buildings in the town, entirely built at Senhor Luiz's own expense. Much of the decoration and all the beautiful texts which lavishly adorned its walls were his own handiwork. On the outside of the building, easily seen by all who enter the town, he had placed a huge carved Bible, inscribed with the words, "Search the Scriptures," and "Repent and believe the Gospel."

---

7. *Ibid.*, p. 82.
8. Ina S. Lambdin, *Trail-Makers in Other Lands*, p. 16.

On the night of my arrival I had the intense satisfaction of preaching to an attentive congregation of several hundreds of people.

This Church has now a membership of over a hundred, and a new building has become necessary.[9]

The same colporteur records several such instances of humanity's recognition of the divine origin of the Book, even where the prevailing attitude is one of distrust of it. For example, he tells of trying to sell a Bible to a farmwoman.

"Senhora," I began, "I have here a very excellent book, the Life of our Lord Jesus Christ. . . ."

"Don't want it," she interrupted, and would have closed the door if I had not casually interposed my foot.

"But you don't know what it is," I rejoined. "It is worth more than all your farm."

"Don't want it," she repeated in a decided tone, for she evidently surmised me to be the terrible *Protestante* who had appeared at Santa Cruz, and she had accepted the priest's story as to my person and the books I circulated.

I endeavored to overcome her prejudice and to interest her in the book, but quite in vain; and finally she exclaimed:

"You are losing your time, senhor. My husband is out, and so I have no money in the house to buy your book."

"Not at all, madam," I replied; "money is no object. Give me a few litres of corn for my horse and you may keep the book."

"Haven't any corn," was the curt reply.

"Never mind that, madam; a couple of litres of *fejiao* (black beans) will do," I suggested, for I knew that beans to a Brazilian are what potatoes are to the Irishman—always at hand.

"Haven't any beans," was the astonishing reply.

"Is that so?—then perhaps a cheese? What?—no cheese? Well, then, give me a sugar brick only and the book is yours."

"Haven't any," was the surly answer, and the case looked hopeless.

Why not give the book? some may say. We have found such to be a very bad policy. *"Livro dado, e livro desprezado"* (A book given is a book despised) is a trite saying among colporteurs; and so we never give, except in cases of real poverty.

9. Frederick C. Glass, *Adventures With the Bible in Brazil*, p. 198.

. . . This, however, does not apply to Gospels, which are very largely given away and attract less enmity.

I was about to turn away in disappointment when, through the half-open door, I caught sight of a dark, unwholesome-looking mass hanging up near the rafters. It was the usual smoked pork fat for culinary purposes.

"Say!" I exclaimed. "Give me half a kilo of that fat and I'll leave you this wonderful book."

With an ill-looking expression on her face the woman picked up a knife, cut off a piece of the greasy stuff, wrapped it up in a banana leaf, and in a very hesitating way received the book in exchange. I rode on quite content with the transaction, and not till some time after did I hear what followed.

In great disgust the woman flung the book in a corner. Shortly after her husband returned, and she at once related how that impertinent *Protestante* had compelled her to buy one of those accursed books, and had walked off with half a kilo of her pig's fat.

"There's the book!" she exclaimed; "have a look at it, and then throw it in the fire—the safest place"; and went out of the room.

Very gingerly the man picked up the book. When he ventured to open it, a verse in the Epistle to the Ephesians caught and held his attention. When his wife returned, nearly an hour later, she was surprised and alarmed to find her husband immersed in the book, and she endeavored to get it away from him.

"No, wife," he cried; "you don't burn this book. Why, it is just the kind of book I have long desired to possess. Just listen to this." And he read her a passage. There was something in what he read that appealed to her, too; so down she sat, and they turned to the first page and began to read through the book.

In the course of a few weeks they had read that Testament through several times, and one day I received a note from the man, whose name was Bellarmino, asking me to pay them a visit.

As I rode out a few days later I reflected on some of the difficulties that awaited me. I remembered the saints and superstitious relics I had noticed on the walls, and I recalled the big rum-still in the backyard. It will be difficult work, thought I, to make quite clear to them that these things must go—especially the latter, an expensive article which he could not conscientiously sell or give away.

On my arrival I was received with smiles by Farmer Bellarmino and his wife. The first thing I noted with surprise was that the objectionable saints had gone, and they told me that they had destroyed the lot—images, crucifixes, and all. The rum-still and the rolls of tobacco had gone too.[10]

It was easy for the missionary-colporteur to lead them to simple trust in Jesus for their salvation from sin. In this case the Bible had brought about a transformed family, a transformed farm, and, subsequently, a transformed district.

In the middle of the last century there was almost no knowledge of the Bible in interior China. Yet, in the experience of Matthew T. Yates, an early Southern Baptist missionary, the people of an inland town found in their hearts a hunger for the message of the first New Testament they had seen.

One day a tea merchant from an interior province came to Yates' church. He seemed interested, and Yates gave him a copy of the New Testament in Chinese. He took it back to his home in the interior. On his next trip he gave Yates a history of the New Testament. The people in the town had literally devoured the Bible and said it was a great and good book. In order to secure more copies they had taken the binding off and distributed the leaves among many writers to copy, until they had sixteen copies of the whole Bible and many copies of portions of it.[11]

It seems that the same marvelous recognition has occurred around the world, regardless of race or background. "In Christ there is no East or West. . . ." Consider the story of Neesima, one of the greatest nineteenth-century Christians in Japan.

One day he borrowed some Chinese books. He opened one of them and read the first sentence. He could hardly believe his eyes. "In the beginning God created the heavens and the earth." Was this the answer to his question? Who was this God? Can you imagine how wonderful the first verse of Genesis would be if you had never read it before? Neesima thought it was the most

10. *Ibid.*, pp. 122–25.
11. Lambdin, *op. cit.*, p. 40.

wonderful thing he had ever read in his life. He longed to have some missionary help him understand this new book, the Bible. But there was no missionary in all that city, which is today the great Tokyo. He begged permission of his father to go to Hakodate, an open port where the foreign teachers lived. His father's answer was a sound thrashing. But after a while, the prince gave him permission to go in one of his ships, and his father had to agree. On March 11, 1864, Neesima said good-by to his home and started toward Hakodate.[12]

At length, Neesima made his way to America on an American ship and was educated here by the kindly owner of the vessel. Returning to Japan, he established a Christian school which came to be one of the most influential institutions of that country. All this because at the first reading he recognized the Bible to be divine truth.

Sometimes Bible-reading groups have appeared in the most unexpected places. Imagine the surprise of a missionary to Syria when he found a whole village studying the Bible.

Mr. Stuart Jessup, a Presbyterian missionary at Sidon, Syria, on one of his trips east of the Jordan River, found an entire village that had been Christianized by one Bible. Twenty years before, one of the villagers was given this Bible while on a business trip to Damascus. Not one in his village at that time knew of Christ and His gospel. This one Bible was read and studied by every family in the village. Scarcely an evening would pass but that a few families would meet in some home to discuss the teachings of this wonderful book. And the villagers gave Mr. Jessup a glad welcome when he arrived at their village, so eager were they to see and hear someone else who believed in their wonderful book.[13]

A similar thing happened in an Asian mountain community.

A merchant from a mountain village in Shansi went to a city on business, and bought from a colporteur on the street a copy of Luke's Gospel. On his return home he so enjoyed the reading of

---

12. *Ibid.*, p. 72.
13. James G. Lawson, *Best Sermon Pictures*, p. 31.

the book that he invited in his neighbours to hear it. After repeated readings, a company of them agreed to give up idol worship, and to observe every seventh day by meeting at the merchant's house for reading and study. The next year the merchant tried to find the colporteur when he went to the city but he was gone. The second year he found a missionary, who explained the difficult passages, and promised to visit his village He found thirty persons ready for baptism, and a large and interested audience was always ready to greet him whenever he could address them.[14]

Mr. Goodchild relates how a Chinese scholar was impressed with the reading of the Bible.

A learned Chinese man was employed by some missionaries to translate the New Testament into Chinese. At first the work of translating had no apparent effect upon the scholarly Chinese. But, after a time, he became quite agitated, and said, "What a wonderful book this is." "Why so?" said the missionary. "Because," said the Chinese man, "it tells me so exactly about myself. It knows all that is in me. The one who made this book must be the one who made me." [15]

Long before the author had collected the evidence in the subsequent chapters of this work he had come to regard the Bible as God's authoritative word to his soul. Perhaps it is well that it is so. The deepest appreciation of the Bible seems to come after a cycle something like this: (1) a man reads it or hears it read and spontaneously recognizes it as God's word; (2) later, arguments arise against this initial intuition; (3) after much soul-searching and study, the man discovers the objective evidence for the supernatural origin of the Bible. After all, this is a standard pattern of successful living. An idea or principle comes to us. We feel it is true. We accept it, use it, and find that it works. When it is called in question, we study it thoroughly and are able to prove its truth logically. It is the contention of this work that when

---

14. *Ibid.*
15. *Ibid.*

a man faces up to the sober realities of human spiritual poverty, if he will give himself to such a reading of the Bible as to grasp its total message, he will instinctively feel it to be the answer of God to the yearnings of his soul. If he then will accept it as such and obey its message, he will find peace for his soul. He may then give himself to critical study of its pages to check his original intuition. If he is patient, he will find a satisfying answer to every doubt which arises. Even the scientist must find his soul's peace in such a way as this. A scientist cannot lay aside his natural investigations to spend fifteen or twenty years in critical study of the Bible before he is ready to trust its message. He, too, must first exercise that God-affinity which is in the heart of every man to recognize the word of God. He then may even condition his acceptance of it upon confirmation by later critical investigation. Every scientist has some philosophy which gives him over-all guidance in the choices of his life. He cannot wait until he is middle-aged to choose one; the choice is forced upon him early. If there is a divine philosophy available to man, why should not the scientist find it early? All philosophies require testing before one can declare confidently, "This is it!" We earnestly commend the philosophy of the Bible as the one most productive of happy, successful living. As for testing the message of the Bible, that Book welcomes it.

Bring ye the whole tithe into the store-house, that there may be food in my house, and prove me now herewith, saith Jehovah of hosts, if I will not open you the windows of heaven, and pour you out a blessing, that there shall not be room enough to receive it.[16]

If any man willeth to do his will, he shall know of the teaching, whether it is of God, or whether I speak from myself.[17]

With the Bible there is no respect of persons. "Except ye turn, and become as little children, ye shall in no wise enter

---

16. Malachi 3:10.
17. John 7:18.

into the kingdom of heaven." [18] God has ordained that in order to enjoy the treasures of heaven, the king, the slave, the elite, the workman, the social outcast, the scientist, and the thief must all humble themselves to the same attitude in order to come into friendship with God—an attitude of recognition and acceptance of the word of God. The long-dormant quality exercised by a Sicilian bandit is essential to every discovery of the Voice of God. Consider

. . . the story of a colporteur who was held at the point of a revolver in a Sicilian forest at dead of night and ordered to light a bonfire and burn his books. Having lit the fire he asked if he might read a brief extract from each book before consigning it to the flames. From one he read the 23rd Psalm; from another the Parable of the Good Samaritan; from another the Sermon on the Mount; from another Paul's hymn of love and so on. After the reading of each extract the brigand exclaimed: "That's a good book; we won't burn that one; give it to me." In the end not a book was burned. They passed one by one into the brigand's hands, who went off, books and all, into the darkness. Years later he turned up again, but this time as an ordained Christian minister, and telling his story to the colporteur he said: "It was the reading of your books that did it." [19]

Most of the time the new convert cannot prove that the Bible is the word of God; but he can say that when he heard its message he felt that it was.

A little Luba-Lulua lad in central Congo sat listening with fixed gaze as the missionary read from the Scriptures. As soon as the service was finished, this small schoolboy hastened to the missionary and asked, "Oh, sir, may I have that book, so that I may read it to the people of my village off in the forest, for those words made holes in my heart." [20]

Perhaps from a practical viewpoint this is the most powerful evidence of all.

---

18. Matthew 18:3.
19. Chirgwin, *op. cit.*, pp. 74–75.
20. From *Spreading the Light,* a leaflet published by the American Bible Society.

CHAPTER II ⋟ *The many various writings pro-*
duced through men of diverse personalities over a
period of fifteen centuries, continually and con-
sistently claim to be of supernatural source. This
fact is unique among religious writings.

THE CLAIMS OF THE BIBLE

T IS OFTEN SAID that the Bible is to be explained as the
result of the natural religious yearnings of men, like the
Bhagavad-Gita of the Hindus, the Koran of the Moslems,
and all other sacred scriptures. Many religious leaders tell
us that experience is the real authority in religion and that
natural human experiences produced the various sacred
scriptures, which later came to be viewed as revealed from
deity. Most of the world's great scriptures, the Bible included, categorically affirm that they are divine revelations.
But when this apparently common character between the
Bible and the other sacred scriptures is examined carefully,
it can be seen that the difference is deeper than the simi-
larity. The others either come from one point in history,
as the Koran, or else the claim of revelation fluctuates
through the centuries, whereas the many various writings
of the Bible, produced through men of diverse personalities
and stations in life over a period of fifteen centuries, continually claim to come from one supernatural source.

(1) The Human Character of Claims
of Other Sacred Books

It is a well-known fact that the authoritative Koran
came from one man, Mohammed, whose adult life scarcely
exceeded twoscore years. There is nothing in the Koran's
claim itself that can be considered evidence for the genuineness of that claim.

There is no homogeneity about the claim of the Egyptia scriptures to being revelation. Although Ikhnaton compose some hymns to the only true god, Aton, most of the othe writings are decidedly polytheistic. Taken as a whole the are a conglomeration—they do not compose a canon o which all the parts have a common source and are in doc trinal agreement.

The real "god" of the Hindus cannot be represente consistently as revealing anything, for he is essentially im personal. Indeed, Krishna and other gods are represented i later Hindu literature as speaking to man, but this is not a in the Bible where all the scriptures claim Jehovah-the-Lor for their author and are in agreement about the great philo sophical questions which have burned in the heart of man While the development of the great aggregate of Hind scriptures lasted many centuries, and they are all looke upon more or less as divine revelations, still the claim of the various scriptures are diverse and often contradic tory. The Rigveda reflects the earliest thoughts of the Arya settlers in India. These thoughts are mostly animistic—the physical world is pervaded by endless sprites. Later the worship of the early Indians took on a more anthropomor phic character and was distinctly polytheistic in some of it scriptures. The next step was to recognize a supreme lorc over all this pantheon, and he was worshiped as the creator But recognizing that everything, including man himself, wa guided by some inward principle, the Indian religious minc came to hold to the idea of an impersonal force as the rea essence of the universe. Thus we have four different idea: incorporated into one body of scripture—animism, polythe ism, quasi-monotheism, and pantheism.[1] One may believe almost anything about deity and still be an acceptable Hindu, providing he conforms to the Hindu social struc ture. And yet divine revelation of some sort is claimed for all this composite structure.

---

1. *Cf.* article "Brahmanism," *Encyclopaedia Britannica*, Vol. 3, p. 1014

Gautama Buddha lived in the fifth century B.C. The third chism of Buddha's followers occurred during the reign of ᴀsoka in the third century B.C. Dr. Edward John Thomas hinks it probable that the Pali Canon was already settled t this time.[2] Thus, not more than two centuries elapsed in he production *and canonization* of the Buddhist scriptures. ince canonization is usually a lengthy process, we may uppose little more than a hundred years for the production ᴏf the authoritative Buddhist scriptures. This is hardly comparable to the consistent and persistent claim of the Bible ᴏ divine origin of its scriptures produced over a period of ᴵfteen centuries. Besides, original Buddhism is decidedly ᴀgnostic if not even atheistic. Its scriptures certainly do not ᴸaim to be inspired by a personal god such as the Jehovah-he-Lord of the Hebrew-Christian scriptures. The Pali ᴄanon is the only one accepted in Ceylon, Burma, and Siam. f one includes the later Mahayana Canon in the Buddhist ᴄriptures, the objection arises that these later scriptures ᴄontain much that is contradictory to the ideas of Buddha ᴴimself. He ignored the gods; these concentrate on them. ᴴe claimed only humanity; these make him a god. The ᴄcriptures of Buddhism cannot make the claim of the Bible ᴏf being one harmonious, though progressive, revelation ʳom one supernatural source over many centuries. The ᴮiblical claim is unique.

In much the same way, the later followers of Zoroaster ᴺade of his religion something very different from what the ᴾrophet intended. He meant for it to be a choice and worship ᴏf the one god of light, Ahura Mazda; they made it a worship ᴏf a host of deities answerable to the various emotional needs ᴏf man. While the original authority for the religion, the ᴀvesta, is on a high spiritual and ethical plane, the later ᴀccretions are polytheistic and often unworthy. Hence, ᴺeither can the scriptures of Zoroastrianism match the

---

2. Article "Buddha and Buddhism," in the *Encyclopaedia Britannica,* Vol. 4, p. 327.

Bible's millennium-and-a-half-long claim to revelation of one kind and of one source.

The scriptures of Confucianism make no pretense at divine origin, at least not in their earlier, most representative form. They simply design to give a man a common sense system of ethics for his happiness in relation to other men. Taoism is evolutionary at the core and "may be considered as the eternal and ubiquitous impersonal principle by which the universe has been produced and is supported and governed." [3] Hence, we would not expect it to exhibit scripture revealed by a personal god. Later Taoism has degenerated to a system of superstition and priestcraft; its scriptures cannot rival those of Christianity.

(2) The Biblical Claims

What then are the claims of the Bible itself? It is surprising to one who has long been familiar with its lofty pages to realize how often it claims for itself a supernatural origin. Each part, in every age through fifteen centuries, has laid title to being the words of the one and only God, Jehovah. Let us trace the development of this unique phenomenon. In order that the reader may see how evenly spaced these claims are throughout the Bible, the references are given in the body of the text.

a) CLAIMS OF A LITERAL WRITING OR VOICE OF GOD.—Exodus 19:19, "And when the trumpet waxed louder and louder, Moses spake, and God answered him by a voice." Exodus 20:22, "And Jehovah said to Moses, Thus thou shalt say unto the children of Israel, Ye yourselves have seen that I have talked with you from heaven." Exodus 31:18, "And he gave unto Moses, when he had made an end of communing with him upon Mount Sinai, the two tables of the testimony, tables of stone, written with the finger of

---

3. W. E. Soothill, *The Three Religions of China*, p. 16, quoted in Edmund Soper, *The Philosophy of the Christian World Mission*, p. 188.

God." Daniel 5:24-25, "Then was the part of the hand sent from before him [God], and this writing was inscribed. And this is the writing that was inscribed: MENE, MENE, TEKEL, UPHARSIN." In the three gospel accounts of the baptism of Jesus, it is claimed that God spoke in a voice from heaven in words like these: "This is my beloved Son, in whom I am well pleased." In John 12:28 it is again claimed that God spoke in an audible voice. In Acts 26:14, Paul avows that the risen Jesus spoke to him "in the Hebrew language."

b) CLAIMS IN THE PENTATEUCH.—Genesis 17:3, "And Abram fell on his face: and God talked with him. . . ." Leviticus begins with the statement, "And Jehovah called unto Moses, and spake unto him out of the tent of meeting, saying . . ." and ends by affirming, "These are the commandments which Jehovah commanded Moses for the children of Israel in Mount Sinai." The book of Numbers begins and ends similarly. Deuteronomy closes by affirming that "Jehovah knew [Moses] face to face."

c) CLAIMS IN THE PROPHETS.—The prophecy of Isaiah is interwoven with a sustained assertion that these are the words of God. In chapter 6 the prophet says, "I heard the voice of the Lord, saying, Whom shall I send, and who will go for us?" Jeremiah 10 begins: "Hear ye the word which Jehovah speaketh unto you, O house of Israel: thus saith Jehovah . . ." Ezekiel begins his prophecy by giving the exact date when "the word of Jehovah came expressly unto Ezekiel the priest, the son of Buzi, in the land of the Chaldeans by the river Chebar: and the hand of Jehovah was there upon him." Daniel claimed a supernatural revelation of the explanation of Nebuchadnezzar's dream. Most of the other prophets certify a supernatural origin for their oracles.

d) CLAIMS IN THE WRITINGS (HAGIOGRAPHA).—The book of Joshua begins with the announcement that "after the death of Moses the servant of Jehovah, Jehovah spake unto Joshua the son of Nun. . . ." The story of Samuel's personal introduction to Jehovah concludes with these words: "And Jehovah appeared again in Shiloh, for Jehovah revealed himself to Samuel in Shiloh by the word of Jehovah." The second book of Samuel states that David received clearcut instructions from God: "And it came to pass after this that David inquired of Jehovah, saying, Shall I go up into any of the cities of Judah? And Jehovah said unto him, Go up. And David said, Whither shall I go up? And he said, Unto Hebron" (II Samuel 2:1). I Kings 9:2 tells that Jehovah appeared unto Solomon and talked with him. According to II Kings 1:3 the angel of Jehovah instructed Elijah to intercept the messengers which the king had sent to enquire of Baal-zebub. The books of Ezra, Nehemiah, and Esther are concerned with certain historical epochs in the affairs of God's people and do not claim supernatural revelation for their writings. These records, however, are intended to give a better understanding of the progress of God's purposes in Israel; and because they do that they were accepted into the canon. The last chapters of Job assert that Jehovah spoke to Job out of a whirlwind. In Psalms 2 and 110 Jehovah is quoted directly. The books of Proverbs, Ecclesiastes, and Song of Solomon are largely the work of Solomon, who, as we have seen, had direct conversation with Jehovah.

e) THE CLAIMS OF JESUS.—Jesus claimed divine authority for both the Old Testament and his own words. In the Sermon on the Mount, Jesus said that "not one jot or one tittle shall pass from the law [the Old Testament] till all be fulfilled"—that is, it was all valid from God. In Mark 7:8–13 he calls the words of Moses the word of God. Speaking of Psalm 110, Jesus asks, "How then doth David *in the Spirit* call him [the Messiah] Lord . . . ?" (Matthew 22:43.) In John 7:16 he says: "My teaching is not mine, but His that sent me." In verse 28 of the next chapter he asserts, ". . . as the Father taught me, I speak these things." Jesus affirms that "the scripture cannot be broken" (John 10:35).

f) CLAIMS OF THE NEW TESTAMENT WRITERS.—Both Matthew and Luke claim to record that "an angel of the Lord" revealed things concerning the coming birth of the Messiah. The Acts of the Apostles records that the Lord spoke unto Ananias in a vision. Paul is very insistent that the gospel which the apostles preach is not from men but from God. "We speak God's wisdom," says he, in I Corinthians 2:7, "in a mystery, even the wisdom that hath been hidden, which God foreordained before the worlds unto our glory." "We speak, not in words which man's wisdom teacheth, but which the Spirit teacheth . . ." (verse 13). He calls the apostles "stewards of the mysteries of God" (4:). "But unto the married I give charge, yea not I, but the Lord, That the wife depart not from her husband . . ." (7:10). In Galatians he says of his gospel: "For neither did I receive it from man, nor was I taught it, but it came to me through revelation of Jesus Christ" (1:12). Peter, in the first chapter of his second epistle, speaks of both pre-Christian and Christian prophets when he says: "For no prophecy ever came by the will of man: but men spake from God, being moved by the Holy Spirit." He claims that the gospel is not composed of cunningly devised Jewish fables, but is attested by eyewitnesses. In 3:15–16 he refers to the writings of Paul as on a par with the Jewish canon. James and Jude were both brothers of Jesus and associates of the apostles, and, therefore, could speak with authority about their teachings. John on Patmos certifies that the real author of the Revelation is Jesus: "He who testifieth these things saith, Yea: I come quickly. Amen: come, Lord Jesus" (22:20).

When Paul affirms in II Timothy 3:16 that "every scripture is inspired of God," he is only drawing up into one grand statement that which the Bible has claimed throughout. The rendering, "every scripture that is inspired of God is also profitable, etc.," is hardly consistent with either Paul's disposition or with the context. Paul is trying to assure Timothy that there is a heavenly guidebook for man's salvation. He would only be heightening Timothy's problem if he had said that men, including the troublemakers, should pick out of the various writings those which appealed to them as God-inspired. Then, too, it is self-evident that "every

God-inspired scripture is profitable." Paul is not given to uttering truisms, especially in such charged contexts as the one in which he was writing in this instance.

(3) The Age of the Bible

It remains to substantiate the contention that the earliest writings of the Bible date in the fifteenth century B.C. The question is, of course, one that has been much debated. Even if the most liberal dating as of the ninth century B.C. be taken, the period over which the writings were intermittently produced is exceedingly long. But to the author's mind, the Pentateuch's age-old claim to Mosaic authorship does not have enough objective evidence against it to warrant serious doubt. Moses is often described therein as writing down various laws and events. While the book of Genesis nowhere claims Moses as its author, the book of Exodus begins with the word "and," and is a natural continuation of the history recorded in the first book. Professor Oswald T. Allis goes on to show that the rest of the Old Testament, the New Testament, Josephus, and the voice of tradition, all affirm the Mosaic authorship.[4] The arguments raised against it are open to objections of the most cogent kind.

a) VARIATIONS IN THE DIVINE NAMES.—Dr. Allis shows that the writer may be intending to emphasize different aspects of God's character in repetition of one of the divine names throughout one passage, and of another name in another passage. He also reduces the criticism to absurdity by pointing out the variety of the use of men's names within documents regarded as units by the higher critics themselves. He also objects tellingly to the appeal to a redactor wherever an uncharacteristic name for God appears in a critical document. He dispels the difficulty of the statement in Exodus 6:3 that Jehovah was "not known" by that name

---

4. *The Five Books of Moses.*

prior to Moses, as indicating simply that Jehovah was not known in his redemptive capacity prior to Moses, though, according to Genesis, the name was at those times recognized as an appellation of God. Again, Dr. Allis exposes the inconsistency of the critics' position by pointing out that in P, wherein Exodus 6:3 appears, Moses' mother's name Jochebed means "Jehovah is glorious."

b) VARIATIONS IN DICTION AND STYLE.—Dr. Allis conclusively demonstrates that these cannot be taken as proof of difference of authorship. In William Robertson's *History of Scotland* are pointed out many parallels to the Pentateuchal variations in style and diction. It is being recognized belatedly in critical study that most of the world's great literary geniuses are capable of quite different styles and choices of words, according to the subject matter, or the writer's mood, or for no apparent reason whatsoever. It is now accepted to be the poorest sort of argument to allege composite authorship because of variations in style and diction of a piece of literature.

c) ALLEGED DOUBLETS.—The repetition of subject matter in a somewhat different manner is characteristic of most poetry and elevated prose, and especially of Hebrew sacred literature. It cannot afford a strong argument against the unity of authorship of a section of the Bible. Dr. Allis multiplies illustrations throughout the Old Testament.

As to the prophets' attitude toward sacrifice, Dr. Allis shows that they assumed the presence of the sacrificial system; and, while they rebuked the hypocrisy that had become connected with it, the idea of a heartfelt and penitent participation in sacrifice received their approval.

d) ARGUMENT FOR THE FIFTEEN-CENTURY EXTENT OF SCRIPTURE.—Moses, the author of the first books of the Bible, lived in the fifteenth century B.C., according to the best chronology. The last books of the New Testament were written near the close of the first century A.D. Hence, we have a period of fifteen centuries during which time a collection of sacred books was produced intermittently by authors of widely differing personalities and stations in life, each insistently, persistently, and consistently claiming his product to be a revelation of the purposes of the one and only God, the Creator, Jehovah, and each writing agreeing with all the rest in doctrinal content. This is hardly what one would expect as a natural result of the evolution of man's religious strivings, for indeed it is a phenomenon that cannot be paralleled from the natural evolution of other religions.

CHAPTER III *There is a humanly inexplicable unity and direction in the movement of thought in the many diverse Scriptures.*

UNITY IN DIVERSITY

IT IS PROPOSED to take a representative cross section of the Bible writers and show that though they lived over a period of fifteen centuries, each carried forward several distinct lines of thought in a way harmonious to all the others. Surely it is evidence of a master intelligence if there was produced a philosophical system of unity and completeness from the writings of many different men of many different ages.

Moses flourished in 1400 B.C., David in 1000, Isaiah in 700, Jeremiah in 600, Zechariah in 500, and Malachi in 400. The New Testament was written in the first century A.D. We will trace the development of several ideas through the writings of this succession of prophets.

a) THE TRANSCENDENCE AND THE IMMANENCE OF GOD.— One of the glories of the Judaeo-Christian doctrine is that it blends in perfect harmony the ideas of the transcendence and the immanence of God. By transcendence, we mean that God is separate from and independent of the universe he has made. By immanence, we mean that God dwells everywhere in and is revealed in the universe around us. Now the wonderful fact is that the Bible consistently teaches that both ideas are true. In Moses' writings we are taught that in the beginning God existed before the universe. After he created it, he had personal fellowship with the man he had created. When man sinned, God drove him out of the paradise he had prepared for him and placed an angel with a flaming sword at the gate thereof to prevent man's return (Genesis 3:24). This certainly bespeaks the transcendence of God. On the other hand, God's self-manifestation through the natural plagues of Egypt bespeaks his immanence (Exodus 7–12). The story of Jacob and the ladder seems to be designed to show that God is present in any place in the world, no matter how remote (Genesis 28:10–17). Moses says: "Lord, thou hast been our dwelling place in all generations," which indicates that God is in all of nature wherein man lives (Psalm 90:1).

David, while often in the Psalms speaking of God as being manifested in natural laws (e.g., Psalm 19), says in the second Psalm that God is able at any time to intervene in the course of human affairs and will do so at a certain crucial time in the future. According to Isaiah, Jehovah has ordained a natural law that peace and prosperity follow from lives that are devoted to dealing justly and mercifully with one's fellow men (56:6–11). Yet Isaiah is pre-eminently a prophet of the transcendence of God. He tells of seeing Jehovah in the temple with ministering cherubim. He speaks of the angel of the Lord destroying 185,000 of Sennacherib's army in order to prevent his attack on Jerusalem. He promises that "Jehovah will come with fire" (66:15) to burn away the evil civilizations of the earth and will create new heavens and a new earth.

Jeremiah is emphasizing the immanence of God when he says (chapter 23): "Am I a God at hand, saith Jehovah, and not a God afar off? Can any hide himself in secret places so that I shall not see him? saith Jehovah. Do not I fill heaven and earth?" In other words, Jehovah has made the world and set it under natural laws, from whose operation none can escape. He has not gone off and left it to run for itself, however, for he is ever-present to interrupt the natural course of events when to do so suits his purposes. "Call unto me, and I will show thee great things, and difficult, which thou knowest not" (33:3). Everywhere he asserts that Jehovah is not bound by the natural course of events but arranges the rise and fall of empires to his own purpose.

Make sharp the arrows, hold firm the shields; Jehovah hath stirred up the spirit of the kings of the Medes; because his purpose is against Babylon, to destroy it: for it is the vengeance of Jehovah, the vengeance of his temple. (51:11)

In the prophecy of Zechariah, Jehovah tells his people that if they will

. . . speak ye every man the truth with his neighbor; execute the judgment of truth and peace in your gates; and let none of you devise evil in your hearts against his neighbor; and love no false oath: for all these are things that I hate . . . there shall be the seed of peace; the vine shall give its fruit, and the ground shall give its increase, and the heavens shall give their dew; and I will cause the remnant of this people to inherit all these things. (8:16–17, 12–13)

The teaching is that God will bless his people through the working of natural principles if they do justly. But at the same time the prophet maintains that when natural laws fail to accomplish God's purpose, he will transcend them; and

. . . then shall Jehovah go forth, and fight those nations, as when he fought in the day of battle. And his feet shall stand in that day upon the mount of Olives, which is before Jerusalem on the east; and the mount of Olives shall be cleft in the midst thereof toward the east and toward the west. . . . (14:3–4)

Malachi promises that if God's people will follow his commands, prosperity and happiness generally will follow:

Bring ye the whole tithe into the store-house, that there may be food in my house, and prove me now herewith, saith Jehovah of hosts, if I will not open you the windows of heaven, and pour you out a blessing, that there shall not be room enough to receive it. And I will rebuke the devourer for your sakes, and he shall not destroy the fruits of your ground; neither shall your vine cast its fruit before the time in the field, saith Jehovah of hosts. And all nations shall call you happy; for ye shall be a delightsome land, saith Jehovah of hosts. (3:10–12)

However, sometimes the opposite works out in this life:

> Ye have said, It is vain to serve God; and what profit is it that we have kept his charge, and that we have walked mournfully before Jehovah of hosts? and now we call the proud happy; yea, they that work wickedness are built up; yea, they tempt God, and escape. (3:14–15)

Consequently Jehovah enrolls the God-fearers in a book and will in due time vindicate them by destroying the wicked with fire of "the great and terrible day of Jehovah" (4:5). Here again we are taught the double truth that though Jehovah works through the laws of nature, his purposes sometimes require that he transcend the natural law.

The New Testament teaches that God has ordained the seasons for man's good and, in general, is the author of order in the universe and not of confusion; but it also teaches that it is necessary that God "hath appointed a day in which he will judge the world in righteousness by the man whom he hath ordained; whereof he hath given assurance unto all men, in that he hath raised him from the dead" (Acts 17: 24–31).

All these different writings maintain alike that while God has ordained that the world should be ordered in general by natural law, he has also declared it necessary for him to intervene at crucial times to carry forward his purposes in the world. In other words, the Bible blends in one grand harmony both the idea of the immanence of God and that of his transcendence, whereas other religious writings tend to overdraw one or the other.

b) THE ESTRANGEMENT OF MAN.—Another unique idea which is developed consistently and completely through the many various Bible authors is that of the estrangement of man. Moses in the book of Genesis tells us that upon man's rebellion against his Creator, God put an angel with a flaming sword to keep Adam out of the Garden of God. David says in the fourteenth Psalm:

Jehovah looked down from heaven upon the children of men, to see if there were any that did understand, that did seek after God. They are all gone aside; they are together become filthy; there is none that doeth good, no, not one.

Far different from the condoning words of the modern positivist preacher are the words of Isaiah the prophet:

Ah sinful nation, a people laden with iniquity, a seed of evil-doers, children that deal corruptly! they have forsaken Jehovah, they have despised the Holy One of Israel, they are estranged and gone backward. (1:4)

Isaiah, as did all the other prophets, called a spade a spade. In one of our newspapers recently, it was said that Jeremiah would have had better success if he had been a better psychologist; he was too blunt with the truth. But it seems that Jeremiah was more under compulsion to deliver himself of the message of God than to be a good psychologist. He speaks for God:

How can I pardon thee; thy children have forsaken me, and sworn by them that are no gods. When I had fed them to the full, they committed adultery, and assembled themselves in troops at the harlots' houses; they were as fed horses roaming at large; every one neighed after his neighbor's wife. Shall I not visit for these things? said Jehovah; and shall not my soul be avenged on such a nation as this? (5:7–9)

Says Zechariah:

Jehovah was sore displeased with your fathers. Therefore say unto them: Thus saith Jehovah of hosts: Return unto me, saith Jehovah of hosts, and I will return unto you, saith Jehovah of hosts. (1:2–3)

Malachi asks:

Will a man rob God? yet ye rob me. But ye say, Wherein have we robbed thee? In tithes and offerings. Ye are cursed with the curse; for ye rob me, even this whole nation. (3:8–9)

The first and third chapters of the book of Romans are the most devastating indictment of human nature that has ever been penned. Consider:

And even as they refused to have God in their knowledge, God gave them up unto a reprobate mind, to do those things which are not fitting; being filled with all unrighteousness, wickedness, covetousness, maliciousness; full of envy, murder, strife, deceit, malignity; whisperers, backbiters, hateful to God, insolent, haughty, boastful, inventors of evil things, disobedient to parents, without understanding, covenant-breakers, without natural affection, unmerciful: who, knowing the ordinance of God, that they that practise such things are worthy of death, not only do the same, but also consent with them that practise them (1:28–32)

It is evident that these many men, each living in a different century, carry forward the same theme. The only logical explanation is that there is a supernatural intelligence moving them to think along the same lines.

c) GOD'S PROVISION OF A SAVIOUR.—The same phenomenon is present with the development of the idea that God would in due time send a Saviour who would rescue men from the power and the penalty of sin. Moses said that the seed of the woman would bruise the head of the serpent (Genesis 3:15). He further states that God told Abram that he purposed to bless all nations of the earth through Abram's seed (Genesis 12:1–3; 18:18–19). David tells that God has ordained that a person worthy of being called David's Lord would sit on the right hand of God, and God would put all wicked enemies under his feet (Psalm 110). Isaiah calls this Promised One God's Servant and says:

Behold my servant shall deal wisely, he shall be exalted and lifted up, and shall be very high. Like as many were astonished at thee (his visage was so marred more than any man, and his form more than the sons of men), so shall he startle many nations; kings shall shut their mouths at him; for that which had not been told them shall they see; and that which they had not heard shall they understand. (52:13–14)

Jeremiah quotes God: "[Israel] shall serve Jehovah their God, and David their king, whom I will raise up unto them" (30:9). And Zechariah wrote:

Rejoice greatly, O daughter of Zion, shout, O daughter of Jerusalem: behold, thy king cometh unto thee; he is just, and having salvation; lowly, and riding upon an ass, even upon a colt the foal of an ass. (9:9)

The last prophet of the Old Testament takes up the strain:

Behold, I send my messenger, and he shall prepare the way before me: and the Lord whom ye seek, will suddenly come to his temple; and the messenger of the covenant, whom ye desire, behold, he cometh, saith Jehovah of hosts (Malachi 3:1)

The whole New Testament is written to tell of the coming of this messenger of the covenant. That is why it is called *he kaine diatheke*—"the New Covenant," or "the New Testament."

We have briefly noticed three themes which have been discussed and developed consistently by six representative authors of the Old Testament and in the New Testament, over a period of fifteen centuries. There is nothing to compare with this phenomenon in all the religious writings of the nations. The Koran was produced mostly by one man in one brief period in history. So was the Avesta, the writings of Confucius, and those of Lao-Tse. The Hindu and Buddhist scriptures cannot show a group of positive doctrines developed consistently by many different authors over a long period of time. The only idea that is consistent with them is one that is obvious—that human life is miserable, and escape lies in the spiritual realm. No other religious writing can show such unity-in-diversity as the Bible.

HISTORICITY

"For we have not followed cunningly devised fables, when we made known unto you the power and coming of our Lord Jesus Christ, but were eyewitnesses of his majesty."—II Peter 1:16

THOSE WHO DO NOT like the message of the Bible have long held it to be full of "cunningly devised fables." The communist governments of the world today in all their power and influence say that it is full of myths. But the most hurtful blow is struck by the avowed lovers of its message who likewise say that its records are myth, legend, folklore, fable, long tradition—in short, anything but historical fact. Typical is a prominent American churchman's comparison of the creation account to the Santa Claus myth.[1] It is a common scholarly viewpoint that Deuteronomy, or the chief element of it, is a "pious fraud," and that the book of Daniel was created centuries after the time from which it professes to come. This is serious. Terrible is the difference that is made whether we base our lives on what we believe is fiction. No morality can long endure that is not based on historical fact. Of the Biblical Adam and Eve story Daniel-Rops has said:

Nothing could be more concise or yet more noble than that brief description of the first pair. A whole psychology, and the whole Western sexual morality, are its fruits.[2]

What will happen to "the whole Western sexual morality" if its source is taken away? Many Christians, whether they know it or not, are retreating into the position of Karl Barth,

---

1. Theodore P. Ferris, *This Created World,* pp. 30 ff.
2. Daniel-Rops, *Sacred History,* p. 65.

who says that it is a matter of no importance to establish the historicity of the Biblical events—that the message of the Bible is *supra-historical*. Here are evangelical Christians who got from the Bible the message of the corrupt nature of man, the eternally fatal wages of sin, the atoning blood of Christ, the regenerating work of the Holy Spirit, and the resurrection of dead bodies at the coming again of Christ, trying to maintain the vitality of that message after they admit that the records producing that message may be fiction. They will not long be evangelical. They have cut away the source of their message.

Why not rather turn the white light of historical research upon the Scriptures and see if these things be so? If they are fiction, then why make so much ado about them? Let us make a thorough study of the true facts of history and guide our lives by these. On the other hand, if the Bible records are true and historical, let us hold them up as the light of a world that is engulfed with heavy gloom.

Our purpose here is primarily to show that the very confirmation of the factual nature of the Bible, as it speaks with certainty about epochs and areas of human experience that otherwise would be shrouded in darkness, is proof of its divine origin. Surely there is something divine about a record that could come down to us, factual and visible, through the centuries, when all other media of recording those momentous events and experiences have been unable to do so. The very incredulity of the knowing world testifies that this is so. The wise men of this world readily affirm that it would be entirely foreign to nature as they know it to take the Bible as factual history: to say that all mankind originated from one man in Mesopotamia; to say that generations later a catacylsmic flood destroyed all human beings except a few who were saved in a boat; to say that the whole human race once lived in one place and spoke one language; to say that over a million Hebrews were sustained alive through forty years of wandering in the Sinaitic wastes; to say that Hebrew prophets lived decades and even centuries ahead of the things which they correctly predicted would befall their people; to say that men wrote down the history of the Jews almost from its beginning; to say that Jesus' followers of his own generation held and propagated a well-organized system of theology—all this, they say, is something other than could conform to the natural evolution of things. Agreed! Then, if these other-than-natural events can be shown to be factual, what a tremendous evidence that factuality (historicity) is to the supernatural origin of the Scriptures!

In modern warfare, it is often recorded that when an enemy had thrown a grenade into a soldier's foxhole, he has picked it up and tossed it back at his enemy. Certain enemies of the authority of the Bible have thrown at us the reproach: "The Bible as you hold it cannot be of divine origin, for it holds so many historical errors" (and by "historical errors" they mean accounts and instances of their transmission which do not fit the nature of things as they know them). In other words, things like those did not happen at the stated times; and if they had happened, the accounts would not have been preserved to us, from the first, in written form. We use their own words against them. "True," we say, "the Bible does contain accounts and instances of their transmission which do not fit the evolutionary pattern; and when we have shown these accounts and instances of their transmission to be actual, then by your own dictum you must acknowledge that the Bible has an other-than-evolutionary origin."

(1) The Antiquity of Writing

There have been always those who hold that the Biblical representation of Moses writing the Pentateuch is hardly worthy of serious consideration. Goodspeed begins a Bible study by saying: "Jewish literature begins with a plea for the poor. It was made by a poor Hebrew workingman of the eighth century before Christ. His name was Amos."[3] Thus

---

3. Edgar J. Goodspeed, *The Story of the Old Testament,* p. 1.

with one fell swoop he disposes of the centuries of Jewish literature which evangelical Christians maintain went before Amos. Professor Allis sees a similar attitude in Albright:

. . . in his *Bible in the Light of Archaeology* (1932), Albright gave as a reason for dating Deut. not earlier than the 10th cty., "the frequent references to writing" and added, "writing was certainly not employed in such cases as divorce contracts (xxiv. 1–4) before the monarchy" (p. 155).[4]

It must be said for the archaeologist that he later modified this view. The desire to make all Jewish writings the culmination of a long tradition has become almost an obsession with many theologians. Some have contended that the Jews had an aversion to writing, greatly preferring the oral method of preserving the records of the nation.[5] It is difficult to see how this can be maintained in full view of the writings of Philo, Josephus, and of the many Jewish apocryphal writers, indeed, of the whole canonical Jewish Old Testament! And why would the Jews repeat through the centuries the same mistake of delaying writing until they knew that the facts in their religious history were in danger of being lost? Would it never occur to them that it would be easier and more effective to record the events soon after they occurred?

Now it appears that not only did the Jews write, but they wrote voluminously, and probably very early in a far-from-pictographic alphabetic script. Several recent discoveries have made it clear that the Israelites could well have used writing in the fifteenth century B.C. Professor Allis points out that the Exodus narrative alludes to the art of writing as a common occupation among the Hebrews of Moses' time:

Five times in Ex. v. allusion is made to the "officers" *(shoterim)* of the Israelites. This word is almost certainly derived from the same root as the Babylonian word "write" *(shataru)* and would

---

4. Oswald T. Allis, *The Five Books of Moses*, p. 337.
5. *Cf.* H. E. Dana, *The Ephesian Tradition*, pp. 11–12.

mean "writers." These "writers" were clearly the men who kept the tally lists of the Israelite workmen who were working for Pharaoh. Such lists have been discovered both in Babylonia and in Egypt.[6]

King David had in his government both the offices of chronicler and secretary.[7]

One of the most important archaeological discoveries of modern times is that of the ewer at Lachish, one of the cities which Joshua destroyed at the time "the sun stood still." On it is an inscription in alphabetic letters similar to Biblical Hebrew. It is thought to be from about 1500 B.C., the time of Moses.

Perhaps the earliest alphabetic script known to modern man (400 years before Moses)[8] was found in a Semitic temple in Sinai, the country where Moses and the children of Israel are stated by the Bible to have lived for forty years. The discoverer, Sir Flinders Petrie, says that the inscriptions show that common workmen of pre-Mosaic times could write, and prove that the Israelites could have used writing.

Another discovery having important bearing upon the antiquity of the Hebrew language is that of the Ras Shamra alphabetic tablets from a temple library of that ancient Mediterranean seaport. Dating from about the fifteenth century B.C., the script is similar to Hebrew in syntax and in the individual peculiarities of many of the words.

Of the fact of pre-Mosaic writing in Palestine, Albright says: "Only a very ignorant person can now suggest that writing (in many forms) was not known in Palestine and the immediately surrounding regions during the entire second millenium B.C."[9]

Now it is known that there were voluminous libraries and systematic language schools in and before Moses' time in

---

6. Allis, *op. cit.*, p. 240.
7. I Chronicles 18:14–17, mg.
8. Henry H. Halley, *The Pocket Bible Handbook*, p. 54.
9. *Ibid.*, p. 55. *Cf.* also Daniel-Rops, *op. cit.*, p. 76: "For at least a thousand years before Abraham, the people of Shinar had known the art of writing."

Egypt, where he grew up, and in Mesopotamia, whence his fathers came. We have legal codes, schoolrooms, dynasty tablets, libraries, dictionaries, grammars, official records, encyclopaedias, works on various arts and sciences, a statue of a scribe, a scribe-town, pre-flood seals, inter-kingdom letters, foundation tablets, a portrait with explanations, victory monuments, an outline of world history, and private documents—all before the time in which Moses is reported by the Bible to have written "the words of this law in a book." [10] We even have writing from before the Great Flood. [11]

The question may well be asked, in view of all this, why should not Moses have written down the founding principles for the new nation? The original and fundamental objection is that it is not in accord with the ideas of gradual development that prevail since the Darwinian revolution. For shame, that modern persons would allow a whole library of facts to be outweighed by a single theory! For one who knows all these facts as to the prevalence of writing in antiquity there is insufficient reason for rejecting the Pentateuchal claim of Mosaic authorship unless he is philosophically predisposed to do so.

(2) Corroboration of Biblical Patriarchs and Peoples

> We search the world for truth. We cull
> The good, the true, the beautiful
> From graven stone and written scroll,
> And all old flower-beds of the soul;
> And, weary seekers of the best,
> We come back laden from our quest,
> To find all the sages said
> Is in the Book our mothers read. [12]

---

10. Deuteronomy 31:24.
11. Halley, *op. cit.*, p. 44.
12. Quoted in *Three Thousand Illustrations for Christian Service,* by Walter B. Knight, p. 31.

In dividing mankind into three major groups, Semitic, Turanian, and Aryan, modern ethnology agrees remarkably with the Table of Nations as given in Genesis 10; yet it is amazing that so little importance has been attached to Biblical information as to early races. If a similar document were discovered in Egypt, scientists would flock to it and it would be minutely studied and reviewed in every ethnological journal in the world. Yet here is a document, purporting to come from remote antiquity and to tell the divisions and subdivisions of the race of man from a common father and mother, and the world's wise men disdain to make use of it. Yet wherever scientific research has spoken at all with regard to references in Genesis to early nations, it has spoken in confirmation. Josephus, who lived two thousand years closer to the events he described than we, elucidated the Biblical Table of Nations in a way that should bring respect of all for the worth of that document.

Let us examine the progressive division of the race as outlined in Genesis 10 and notice how well the Biblical account is corroborated by other notices as to the ancient settlements of nations. The author does not pretend that all these possible identifications are actual. No doubt some are mere coincidence; but enough of them are substantiated to give credence to the account as a whole.

The Table of the Nations (Gen. 10)

Noah was survived by only three sons: Shem, Ham, and Japheth.

I. Japheth. "The Greeks had a tradition that 'Iapetos' (Japheth?) was the father of the human race." [13]

    A. Gomer. The sound of the name is preserved in the Armenian word *Gamir* (cf. Assyrian *Gimirrai*), meaning Cappadocia, and in Homer's Cimmerii. Josephus says that the Galatians were formerly called Gomerites.[14]

---

13. Halley, *op. cit.*, p. 80.
14. William Whiston, *The Life and Works of Flavius Josephus*, p. 40.

The Celts, or Gauls, or Galatians,[15] settled in Asia Minor and later in France (called Gaul by Julius Caesar) and in the British Isles. Also, there is a large administrative city in White Russia called Gomel. White Russia is so called from the lightness of the skins of its inhabitants, a characteristic of the Celtic group.

1. Ashkenaz. Josephus takes him to be the father of the Rheginians.[16] The Jews call the Germans Ashkenazites.

2. Riphath.

3. Togarmah. In ancient times the Armenians were called "the House of Togarmah." [17]

B. Magog. Josephus says the Scythians came from him.[18]

C. Madai. Media, later called Persia and now called Iran—that is, Aryan, since its people were Aryans. You will remember that modern ethnology makes one of the three primitive peoples Aryan.

D. Javan. His name is preserved in that of the Ionians, who settled Greece—that is, "the islands and/or coastlands of the Gentiles." Perhaps the Scandinavian name Ivan is also related.

1. Elisha. Compare the Greek "Elysian fields." Josephus makes him founder of the Aeolians. [19]

2. Tarshish. From him we get the name of the great Greek university city Tarsus, where Paul was educated. Also, a section of the coast of Spain was once called Tarshish.

3. Kittim. Josephus tells us that the island of Cyprus was formerly called Cethima, and that there was in his own day a city there named Citius.[20]

4. Dodanim. The parallel tables in I Chronicles 1:7

---

15. Ernest Burton, *The Epistle to the Galatians*, p. xvii: "Greek authors use the terms *Keltoi, Keltai,* and *Galatai;* Latin authors the similar terms *Celtae, Galatae,* and *Galli,* without clear discrimination."

16. Whiston, *loc. cit.*

17. Harry Rimmer, *The Shadow of Coming Events*, p. 111.

18. Whiston, *loc. cit.*

19. *Ibid.*

20. *Ibid.*

(R.V.) and in LXX both read "Rodanim" here. These Brown, Driver, and Briggs identify as the Rhodians, who built the famed colossus of the ancient world.

E. Tubal. Deep in eastern Russia there is a river named Tobol. Remember that primitive Hebrew had no vowel signs, so that, as far as the consonants go, Tubal is identical with Tobol. Situated on this river is the key city of Tobolsk. Thobel is known as the patriarch of the Iberes, from whom the Iberian Peninsula (Spain) was named.

F. Meshech. Brown, Driver, and Briggs make this word cognate with "Moschi"—that is, the Muscovites, from whom Moscow got its name. The ancient Assyrians located them in west or north Armenia, and the ancient Persians held them to be settled farther northeast. At any rate, the indication is that they settled in what is now Russia. According to Josephus, the Mosocheni, or Cappadocians, had in his day a city called Mazaca.[21]

G. Tiras. Founder of Tyre and, according to Josephus, father of the Thracians.[22]

II. Ham. In ethnology a Hamite is a member of the chief native race of North Africa, of dark skin.

A. Cush. In Josephus' time the Ethiopians were called Cushites.[23] Although they have a strain of semitic blood (the emperor claims descent from Solomon and Bathsheba), they are still recognized as Hamitic. The Cushites are favorably mentioned in the *Iliad*.

1. Seba. The land of Seba is situated "most probably . . . on the West coast of the Red Sea."[24] Ancient Saba was in southern Arabia. The Sabean language was similar to Hebrew.

2. Havilah.

3. Sabtah.

4. Raamah.

   a) Sheba.

   b) Dedan.

5. Sabtachah.

---

21. *Ibid.*

22. *Ibid.*

23. *Ibid.*

24. Brown, Driver, and Briggs, *A Hebrew and English Lexicon*, p. 685.

6. Nimrod. Near Nineveh is a ruined city called "Nimrud." Layard says, ". . . tradition still points to the origin of the city, and, by attributing its foundation to Nimrod, whose name the ruins now bear, connects it with one of the first settlements of the human race." [25] It is interesting to note that the name Nimrod has been identified with the name of the early Babylonian god Marduk.

B. Mizraim. It is clear that the Hebrew place-name Mizraim refers to Egypt. Josephus says, "We call Egypt Mestre." [26]

   1. Ludim.

   2. Anamim.

   3. Lehabim. According to Josephus, Libya got its name from them.[27] They are probably the same as the Lubim mentioned elsewhere in the Bible. On a stele of Susa the victory of Naram-Sin, a Babylonian king, over "the Lulubu," the mountain people, is depicted. Could this be the Lehabim?

   4. Naphtuhim.

   5. Pathrusim. Inhabitants of Pathros, or Upper (southern) Egypt.

   6. Casluhim, ". . . out of whom came Philistim"—that is, the Philistines, from whom Palestine was named They were probably first settled in Crete. We know that they came to Canaan to get grain.

   7. Caphtorim. These are Cretans, according to Brown, Driver, and Briggs.[28]

C. Phut. Libya was formerly called Phut. Perhaps he and his nephew Lehab were its co-settlers.

D. Canaan. From him come the Canaanites and the name of the land of Canaan.

   1. Sidon. Note the city of Sidon in Canaan, on the Mediterranean.

   2. Heth. Out of the past the archaeologist has resur-

25. C. W. Ceram, *Gods, Graves and Scholars*, pp. 243–44.
26. Whiston, *loc. cit.*
27. *Ibid.*
28. *Op. cit.*, p. 499.

rected the mighty empire of the Hittites, though formerly it was denied that they even existed.

3. Jebusite.
4. Amorite. Archaeology tells us that the Amorites and the Hittites mingled to form the people known as the Canaanites.
5. Girgashite.
6. Hivite.
7. Arkite.
8. Sinite. Perhaps Sin gave his name to the Sinaitic Peninsula. Who knows if he did not also give his name to the ancient Sinic (Chinese) civilization? Too, the word *sin* appears often on Babylonian monuments and tablets.
9. Arvadite.
10. Zemarite.
11. Hamathite. The name persists in the present village of Hama, north of Damascus. In the first century it was called Amathe.[29]

III. Shem. The Semitic division of mankind is recognized by almost all.

A. Elam. He gave his name to the Elamites, or Persians.
B. Asshur. We see his name in Assyria and that of the Assyrians.
C. Arpachshad. The progenitor of the Chaldeans, according to Josephus.[30]

   1. Salah.

     a) Eber. His name means "passenger," and it was from him that the Hebrews got their name. It is doubly fitting, because the Hebrews did come from across "the River" (Euphrates), and also, they were passengers through the Red Sea.

       (1) Peleg—"Division." In his time the nations were divided.

       (2) Joktan. Josephus says that his sons inhabited India. However, several traces of their names seem to be found in Arabia.

---

29. Whiston, *op. cit.*, p. 41.
30. *Ibid.*

      (*a*) Almodad.
      (*b*) Sheleph.
      (*c*) Hazarmaveth. "Now Hadramaut, a district in southern Arabia, somewhat east of Aden." [31]
      (*d*) Jerah.
      (*e*) Hadadoram.
      (*f*) Uzal
      (*g*) Diklah.
      (*h*) Obal.
      (*i*) Abimael.
      (*j*) Sheba. Sabean is a language similar to Hebrew. Saba was in southern Arabia. In view, however, of Josephus' statement,[32] perhaps these came from the Seba who was the first son of Cush.

D. Aram. The Aramaic language and the Aramaeans bear witness to his name. Now they are called Syrians.
  1. Uz. He founded Damascus, according to Josephus.[33]
  2. Hul. Founder of Armenia.[34]
  3. Gether. Progenitor of the Bactrians.[35]
  4. Mash. Father of the Mesaneans.[36] Perhaps his name is preserved in that of Mes-annipadda, who was the father of A-annipadda, king of Ur, according to a foundation tablet found by Woolley near Ur. Since Mes-annipadda appears in a very ancient king-list as founder of the third dynasty after the Flood, his date would suit that of the Biblical Mash.

While some of these identifications are highly conjectural, most of them have considerable substance to them, as, for instance Mizraim—Egypt, Aram—Syria, Elam—Persia, Shem—Semites, Asshur—Assyrians, Eber—Hebrews, Phut—Libya, Heth—Hittites. Canaan—Canaan, Cush—Ethiopia,

31. M. F. Unger, *Archaeology and the Old Testament*, p. 98.
32. Whiston, *loc. cit.*
33. *Ibid.*
34. *Ibid.*
35. *Ibid.*
36. *Ibid.*

Tiras—Tyre, Meshech—Muscovites, Javan—Greece, Madai—Media. The very fact is astounding that there is in existence an extremely ancient document which attributes the sounds of the names of most primitive peoples to three brothers and their near offspring. Truly, this makes even more plausible the statement of one of the greatest linguists of our day:

> The languages of men probably go back to a common origin, but that origin is lost to modern men. The late Alfredo Trombetti of Rome (*The Unity of Origin of Language*) claimed to be able to prove this to be a fact.[37]

This compilation of identifications is not complete; but it is nearly enough complete to show that the author of Genesis 10 had a comprehensive grasp of the ancient peoples of the world; and it offers the best working outline of the relation of the nations about which the author knows anything. Among the many various and often conflicting outlines noted in the encyclopedic articles, none gave such a clear and comprehensive picture as does the Table of the Nations in Genesis.

(3) Corroboration of Biblical Place-Names

Biblical writers seem to have had an obsession to situate their narratives in history. Genesis, the Old Testament book whose historicity is perhaps most often assailed, includes fifty references to place-names in the first fourteen chapters, most of which are now known to be existing or likely to be existing at the times indicated. The Fourth Gospel, most often charged with unhistoricity in the New Testament, contains the most historical references of all the New Testament books. It seems sometimes the author was going out of his way to indicate the actuality of his narratives. In them he indicates the time of day, of the week, of the year, and the time in relation to Jewish feasts; who was related

---

37. A. T. Robertson, *A New Short Grammar of the Greek New Testament,* p. 3.

o whom; the home towns of various disciples; the place
whence and the place whither; the fact that Jesus himself
did not baptize; the customs and prejudices of various sec-
ions and cities of Palestine; two historic shrines at Sychar;
the number of porches a Jerusalem pool has, and by what
gate it lies; the alternate name of the Sea of Galilee; the
number of loaves and fish a boy's lunch contained; how
many baskets of fragments remained at a mass feeding;
courses of shipping on the Sea of Galilee; the meaning of
various place-names; the character and habits of the Sanhedrin in the early first century; the situation of sections of
the temple area; the character of certain cities; the price of
perfume; the customs and etiquette of the Jews and of fisher-
men; the brook which must be crossed to get from Jerusalem
to Gethsemane; the name of the high priest's servant; the
actual political situation of the high-priesthood; the kind of
fire the officers made; the makeup of Pilate's judgment hall;
the three languages of crime notices; the customs of crucifixion; the weight and composition of an embalming mixture;
nicknames; the distance a ship was from shore; the number
of fish in a catch and the distinction between fresh and
pickled fish. The book contains a certification that John the
apostle wrote it.

The book of Genesis claims to be a history of events that
no other writing extant delineates with parallel completeness. What of its references to various place-names? Are
they accurate? Are they chronistic? Let us examine some
of them. It is not necessary positively to identify each place
in the times. If we can show that conditions were such at
the time of the narrative that the said places could have
existed as stated, then the burden of proof falls on him who
would reject their historicity.

By account of the narrative itself the pre-Flood civilizations would be obliterated. Hence, it is not necessary to identify Eden or Nod, or the two smaller rivers, Gihon and
Pishon, which may have been altered by the Flood. It may
be pointed out, however, that the name of man's first home

persists in an ancient settlement on the southwest coast o
the Arabian Peninsula, Aden, formerly Adana. " 'Edin' wa
the ancient name of the Babylonian plain." [38] The writer'
references to the Tigris ("Arrow") and Euphrates ("Cii
cuitous") rivers agree with what we know of pre-Ham
murabic geography.

Ancient Assyria, shrouded in mist until our modern era
now emerges as a flesh-and-blood tyrannical empire, an
that, one of the first. Now it is known that Assyria wa
colonized from Babylon just as Genesis 10 states.

In eastern Turkey are "the *mountains* of Ararat" (Gene
sis 8:4): Little Ararat, about 13,000 feet, and Great Arara
about 17,000. The latter was scaled in 1829. Tradition say
Noah's ark landed here. The earliest settlers of India wer
Aryans from this vicinity.

Babel, Erech, Accad, Calneh, Nineveh, and Calah (nov
called Nimreud) have all been positively identified. Who
ever wrote this account was well informed as to the geog
raphy and history of the times about which he wrote. Erec
is prominently mentioned in the Chaldean genesis account
as Urak. It is now called Warka. "It was ravaged by Kudu
nan-khunte, king of Elam, in the year 2280 B.C., accore
ing to an inscription of Assurbanipal (670 B.C)." [39]

Excavations of the ruins of Babylon extended throug
most of the nineteenth century. In the center of the ruins
a tower on which an inscription was found:

The building of this illustrious tower offended the gods. In
night they threw down what they had built. They scattered the
abroad, and made strange their speech. Their progress the
impeded. They wept hot tears for Babylon.[40]

The tower was about 300 feet square and about 300 fee
high. On its summit was a sanctuary to Marduk, the ver

38. Henry H. Halley, *The Pocket Bible Handbook*, p. 64.
39. R. Payne Smith, in *The Handy Commentary, Genesis*, p. 1
(Chas. Elliott, editor).
40. Halley, *op. cit.*, pp. 82–83.

ancient god of the Babylonians, whose name is possibly the equivalent of Nimrod, who built the city, according to the Genesis account. Why is it so hard to accept the claim of the writer of Genesis that he was writing historically?

Describing the finding of the tower, Ceram says:

Koldeway actually excavated only the great base of the Tower, which none the less had once existed, as described in the Bible. The original structure was probably razed as early as the reign of Hammurabi, and at a later date another "tower" was built in memory of the first.[41]

He goes on to quote Nabopolassar to the effect that at Marduk's command he rebuilt the "Tower of Babel," which had become "weakened by time." This indicates a state of great antiquity for the Tower at the time of Nabopolassar, who lived six hundred years before Christ. Tukulti-Ninurta I of Assyria broke down the Tower around 1250 B.C. There is nothing unlikely about the Bible account of a Babylon built hundreds of years before the time of Hammurabi and Abraham. The scriptural record of Nineveh's being colonized from Babylon is also corroborated by the inscriptions.

Perhaps for "the city Rehoboth" in Genesis 10 we should understand "the suburbs of the city," that is, of Nineveh. If so, it further magnifies that city in the account of the Genesis writer. Its magnitude is vouched for by modern scholarship, though its ruin was such that Alexander the Great passed within sight of the place without knowing of its presence.

Sidon was the capital of ancient Phoenicia. It is now a seaport in southwest Lebanon. Notice in Genesis 10 that Sidon is given as the northern limit of the Canaanites. Hamath and Aradus, however, cities named after two of Canaan's sons, were far to the north of Sidon. Hence, we are to understand that the writer is giving information as to a much earlier situation of the peoples of Canaan.

---

41. C. W. Ceram, *Gods, Graves, and Scholars*, p. 288.

There are many evidences that there was formerly a flourishing culture in the vicinity of the Dead Sea. Certainly the references to bitumen substantiate the author's accuracy as to the region. To this day there is abundance of bitumen at each end of the Dead Sea. During earthquakes great quantities have come to the surface. There is a mountain named Usdom (Sodom) at the southwest corner of the Dead Sea. Josephus tells us that there was in his day a city called Zoar, being the remnant of the one to which Lot fled at the destruction of Sodom, Gomorrah, Admah and Zeboim, cities of the plain.[42]

A few generations ago the word Accad was meaningless; now it is one of the terms most often used in Assyriology. Many of the Assyrian inscriptions reflect a language anterior to the Semitic culture of Chaldea. At great length it has now become apparent that this language is Accadian, from the people who settled the area before the Assyrians.

Of Shinar, Hestiaeus, the Greek historian, says: "Such of the priests as were saved [from the Flood?] took the sacred vessels of Jupiter Enyalius, and came to Shinar of Babylon." [43] The plain of Shinar probably gave its name to the Sumerians, whose culture is perhaps the oldest of which we have enough relics to describe. The Sumerians are well known to the student of antiquity. Muir suggests that Shinar is the Singar on the eastern branch of the Euphrates.[44]

At Ur, Leonard Woolley, the English archaeologist, discovered abundant remains of what has been termed the oldest culture in the world—the Sumerian. Abraham's home town was a flourishing city with indoor plumbing, schoolhouses, libraries, temples and palaces. It was a seaport on the Persian Gulf at the mouth of the Euphrates, and also a center of manufacture, farming, and land trade. Before Abraham's birth, Queen Shubab of Ur and her ladies wore elab-

---

42. Whiston, *op. cit.*, p. 47.
43. Quoted by Josephus, *ibid.*
44. James C. Muir, *The Spade and the Scriptures*, p. 29.

orate headdress, beads, necklaces, gold, silver, semi-precious stones, and cosmetics. Why should not Abraham have actually migrated from such a place to go into the land of Canaan?

Archaeologists tell us that the land of Canaan was settled by the Amorites and later by the Hittites, who amalgamated to become the Canaanites. This reminds us of what Ezekiel said to Jerusalem: "Thy birth and thy nativity is of the land of Canaan; thy father was an Amorite, and thy mother a Hittite." [45]

Haran was "the Half-way House" of the primitive world, located at the crest of the fertile crescent extending in an arc northwestward from Ur along the twin rivers to the Levant and then southwestward to Egypt. Now it is called Carrhae and is about twenty miles from Edessa.

Shechem means "shoulder" and is the name of the ridge joining Mounts Ebal and Gerizzim. Since the name comes from the natural configuration of the place, there is nothing unlikely about its being very ancient, as the author of Genesis indicates.

Bethel, ten miles north of Jerusalem, is on the watershed of the Judaean country. You will remember that Jerusalem is on a ridge of high land that runs north and south between the Mediterranean and the Jordan. From here there was a grand view of the surrounding countryside, especially the Jordan valley. There is nothing unnatural in the story that from this place Lot "beheld all the plain of Jordan that it was well watered everywhere . . ." [46] and thus separated from his uncle, Abram.

The extreme southern section of Palestine is still called the Negeb. Dr. Nelson Glueck, President of Hebrew Union College, has recently done three months study in the Negeb. He holds that his findings support the Bibilical references to the region. [47]

---

45. Ezekiel 16:3.
46. Genesis 13:10.
47. *St. Louis Post Dispatch*, Sept. 17, 1954.

Ellasar is Al-Larsa, that is, the City of Larsa, famous in archaeological circles. It is now called Senkereh.

Concerning the Vale of Siddim at the Salt Sea, it is reported that the Arabs still call the cliffs at the southern edge of the plain of Jericho "sidd." [48]

The ruins of Ashteroth-Karnaim are seen at Tell-Ashtereth in the Hauran.

Genesis speaks of ". . . the Horites [cave-men] in their Mount Seir." Now it is known that the primitive cave-dwellers of the mountainous region south of Canaan were driven out by the Edomites, who left us the fine rock city and culture of Petra. [49]

En-Mishpat (Kadesh) ". . . was a great stronghold, and both a sanctuary and seat of government. It has been visited lately by Mr. Trumbull, for whose account see Palestine Exploration Fund, Quarterly Statement, July 1881, pp. 208–212." [50]

Salem is Jerusalem, known to be a very ancient city. It is not at all unlikely that the earliest inhabitants of southern Canaan chose the site as their center, for it dominated the whole region and was easily fortified so as to be well-nigh impregnable.

We have examined only two Biblical books in this place-name study; and yet what is true of Genesis and the Fourth Gospel is true in general of the rest of the Scriptures—they are full of references to the historical situation, references which can stand the glare of intense criticism.

(4) Vindication of Biblical Statements on Early Events and Conditions

Those who reject the actuality of Bible history have a long list of impossible Bible incidents and situations, many of which have become hackneyed through the years. Now

---

48. Smith, *op. cit.,* p. 183.
49. Harry Rimmer, *Dead Men Tell Tales,* pp. 225 ff.
50. Smith, *op. cit.,* p. 185.

they are teaching the children to view the Scriptural accounts as imaginative. In a Bible-story book for the very young one such teacher says:

The Book of Genesis was written because hundreds and hundreds of years ago people asked questions, just as we do now. They looked at the world around them and at all the marvelous things in the sky and on the earth, and they wondered how everything had come to be the way it was. It could not just have happened, they said, God must have made it all. Then they went on wondering about God and his way of working when he made the world. And what they thought and what they wrote is what we can read in the first pages of the Book of Genesis.[51]

And another says: "Pupils may later discard the scientific import of the story" (of the creation).[52] Many years previously Wellhausen had taught those who are now teachers:

That four kings from the Persian Gulf should, "in the time of Abraham," have made an excursion into the Sinaitic Peninsula, that they should on this occasion have attacked the five kinglets on the Dead Sea littoral and have carried them off prisoners, and finally that Abraham should have set out in pursuit of the retreating victors, accompanied by 318 men servants, and have forced them to disgorge their prey—all these incidents are sheer impossibilities, which gain nothing in credibility from the fact that they are placed in a world which has passed away.[53]

In a similar fashion he disposes of the Biblical picture of the Hittites as the imaginative expansion of a small tribe into imperial proportions.

Long is the list of charges against Biblical historicity. Among them are objections to scriptural accounts of the creation, the fall, the flood, Abraham, Moses, Israel, Joshua, the sacrificial system, stories of crime, Saul's failure to recog-

---

51. Walter R. Bowie, *The Bible Story for Boys and Girls, Old Testament,* p. 9.

52. Prof. O. F. Nolde, quoted by T. Engelder, *The Scripture Cannot Be Broken,* p. 10.

53. Quoted by Engelder, *op. cit.*

nize David, axeheads floating, Elisha and the she-bears, Jonah, Belshazzar, Quirinius, Jesus' genealogies, resurrection from the dead, "misquotations," and "discrepancies." Many of these charges are found almost verbatim in Celsus (A.D. 180), the most famous early opponent of Christianity, in Porphyry (latter third century) and in Voltaire, Paine, and Ingersoll. These men sought by frontal attack to dispose of Christianity. Said Voltaire: "In twenty years, Christianity will be no more. My single hand shall destroy the edifice it took twelve apostles to rear." [54] Bruno Baer and Wellhausen and other Christian teachers faced these objections and decided that they were truth. They felt that Christianity, which had so long and so successfully contended with them, should admit their truth and still retain that which was essential in the Christian message. As one modern Christian teacher put it, he must retreat into the citadel of the core of Christianity. After examining dozens of these originally heathen charges of error in the Bible, and finding a reasonable answer to each of them, this author is convinced that the modern critics have not been critical enough in their appraisal of the objections to the inspired accuracy of the Bible. For example, take the one that Quirinius was not governor of Syria at the time of the census connected with the birth of Jesus, as Luke states. A little critical knowledge of history would tell one that Quirinius was governor in A.D. 6. Further critical study would bring to light Tertullian's statement that Sentius Saturnius was governor of Syria, 9–6 B.C. The papyri indicate the census would begin 8 B.C. and be repeated every fourteen years. Here the critics stopped. Luke is wrong in stating that Quirinius was governor: But a little more critical investigation would have shown that Tertullian was speaking loosely, for inscriptions show that others were managing the internal affairs of Syria at the time of Christ's birth while Quirinius, the official governor, was busy at the head of the army. Thus, if we allow for a

---

54. W. B. Knight, *3000 Illustrations for Christian Service,* pp. 230–31.

little probable delay for the census to be completed in Palestine, there is nothing wrong with Luke's statement. In case after case the critics have been not critical (careful) enough in their acceptance of charges of error in the Bible.

Let us critically examine some of the charges made against the historicity of the statements claimed for Moses in the Pentateuch. Moses clearly indicates that the birthplace of the human race is in Mesopotamia, "the land between the [Tigris and Euphrates] rivers." Those who consider it a mark of intellectual honesty to favor a contradiction of the Scriptures have long contended for a beginning in Egypt, China, or India. But scientific investigation tends toward a later development in Egypt than is commonly supposed [55] and an earlier development in Mesopotamia. As Professor J. McKee Adams of the Southern Baptist Theological Seminary has said:

Now, apart from numerous theories concerning the place of man's beginning, it is urged at this point that the Genesis narrative and modern opinion practically agree in associating the inception of human culture with a country of abounding rivers and an environment favorable to primitive conditions. It is generally accepted that Mesopotamia meets that description better than any other section of the Biblical world of which we now have knowledge.[56]

This region is admirably suited to a primitive society, being in the same latitude as our own Southland. The several rivers would provide the earliest inhabitants with an abundance of water and a ready means of transportation. As the society grew, irrigation would be easy, for the Tigris and

---

55. *Cf. The Encyclopaedia Britannica,* Vol. 8, p. 43: "We think that the First Dynasty began not before 3400 and not much later than 3200 B.C. . . . the most generally accepted date is *c.* 3200 B.C. (Meyer)." *Cf.* Ceram, *op. cit.,* p. 302: "Even the most conservative Assyriologists had to admit that some of the newly discovered [by de Sarzec in Mesopotamia] stone fragments dated back to 4000 and 3000 B.C., to a culture older than the Egyptian."

56. J. McKee Adams, *Biblical Backgrounds,* pp. 26–27.

Euphrates beds are higher than the surrounding land. Evidence abounds that those early people did make a fine network of canals. While it is not positively demonstrated that Mesopotamia is the seat of earliest culture as Genesis states, our investigation thus far indicates that there is nothing improbable about the statement as far as general suitability is concerned.

Dr. Adams holds that the earliest tombs at Ur antedate the first Egyptian dynasty by several centuries.[57] Dr. Howells, Professor of Anthropology at the University of Wisconsin, who is certainly not a Biblicist, holds that:

Greece and Rome, indeed, tended to look on Egypt as the mother of civilization, but they certainly gave her too great a share of the credit, for she drew on older sources in common with Sumer, and continuously thereafter on the Near East and Mesopotamia.[58]

Of the earliest civilization in India, the Harappa, he says that it doubtless had some impulse from Mesopotamia or Persia. He feels that the same impulses that brought civilization to Mesopotamia and India reached China centuries later.

Now, Genesis 11:2 states that the early people came to Shinar from the east. Perhaps when they found themselves disembarked in the vast loneliness of the Armenian highlands, they spent considerable time wandering eastward along the mountain system which runs from Turkey to Tibet, fearing for a long time to descend to the lowlands to the south in view of the terrible experience of the Deluge. We may imagine them migrating as far eastward as the Indus valley and settling there for a while. At last the memory of the pleasant living in Mesopotamia overcame their fear and they found their way back to the original home of the race.

This theory resolves the dilemma which Ceram found between the fact of the mountain-consciousness of the

---

57. *Ibid.*, pp. 36–37.
58. Wm. Howells, *Back of History*, p. 336.

Sumerians and their traditions of having come into Mesopotamia from the sea. Their sea-consciousness would come
from the year-long residence in the ark. Other facts are
satisfied by this theory. The study of the origins of races
and languages points to the region of the highlands of south
central Asia. According to Sir Arthur Keith:

One can still trace the ancient Sumerians eastwards among the
inhabitants of Afghanistan and Baluchistan, until the Valley of
the Indus is reached, some 1500 miles distant from Mesopotamia.[59]

The remains of a people of a culture similar to the Sumerians
have been discovered in the Indus valley. "The Sumerian
language is somewhat similar to Turkish, or Turanian." [60]
The Turanians are those who inhabited these very mountainous regions we have been discussing.

Perhaps the most telling authoritative statement which
supports the Biblical narrative is that of Woolley:

Their civilization, lighting up a world still plunged in primitive
barbarism, was in the nature of a first cause. We have outgrown
the phase when all the arts were traced to Greece, and Greece
was thought to have sprung, like Pallas, full-grown from the
brain of the Olympian Zeus; we have learnt how that flower of
genius drew its sap from Lydians and Hittites, from Phoenicia
and Crete, from Babylon and Egypt. But the roots go farther
back; behind all these lies Sumer.[61]

All this, then, makes very plausible the Mosaic statement
that civilization began in Mesopotamia. While the evidence
is not conclusive, it is enough to dissipate the charge that
the Genesis account is not realistic.

---

59. Quoted by Ceram, *op. cit.,* p. 315.
60. *Ibid.,* p. 313.
61. *Ibid.,* p. 320. *Cf.* W. F. Albright: "Archaeological research has
thus established beyond doubt that there is no focus of civilization in the
earth that can begin to compete in antiquity and activity with the basin
of the Eastern Mediterranean and the region immediately to the east of it
—Breasted's Fertile Crescent"; quoted by Merrill F. Unger, *Archaeology
and the Old Testament,* p. 40.

With the anti-Biblicist it is usually assumed, though not proved, that the Bible story of a civilization-wide flood is a campfire story taken up and expanded to meet the design of the author of the account in Genesis. Ceram says:

Naturally, this actual flood, which gave rise to the Deluge as myth, did not destroy the whole human race with the exception of Ut-napishtim–Noah and family. It must have been an unusually severe example of the characteristic local inundations that periodically drown the Euphrates-Tigris delta region.[62]

When he says "naturally" he means in view of the prevailing scholarly feeling that excludes such a catastrophic event. But the facts Ceram has already enumerated point the other way: (1) an 8.2-feet-thick alluvial deposit discovered by Woolley at Ur; (2) the correspondence between the Biblical story and the Gilgamesh epic;[63] (3) the Sumerian king-lists' recognition of the flood; and (4) repeated validation of old legends and Bible lore by archaeology.

Another Babylonian flood story concerns one Xisuthrus. The Xisuthrus epic and the Biblical flood account contain too many points of identity to have had separate origins: (1) the Deluge was caused by the Deity as judgment on sin; (2) Deity initiated the building of the ship; (3) the rescue vessel was very large (450 feet in Genesis; 900 feet in Xisuthrus); (4) it was in the nature of a house; (5) seed of all animals and birds was preserved; (6) Deity indicated the time to enter the ship; (7) it was sealed with bitumen; (8) there was an earthquake in connection with the flood; (9) all living things were destroyed off the land; (10) the rain was long and tremendous; (11) the ship rested on a mountain; (12) a dove and a raven were sent out; (13) on his departure from the ship the hero sacrificed animals; (14)

---

62. Ceram, *op. cit.*, p. 313.
63. *Cf. ibid.*, p. 276: "There are, of course, flood stories in almost every folklore, but this one was concerned with the very same deluge described, at a later date, in Genesis. Ut-napishtim, indeed, was none other than Noah."

the rainbow was the sign of amnesty; and (15) repetition of the flood was renounced.

Even the Egyptians bear witness that Egypt is not the cradle of civilization, for one of the ancient records tells about a great flood which wiped out all mankind except some wandering shepherds, who escaped by climbing the mountains of Armenia with the help of the gods. Similar traditions are found among the Greeks, Hindus, Chinese, Druids, Polynesians, Mexicans, Peruvians, American Indians, and Greenlanders. Dr. Ingstadt learned the story thus from an old man of the Nunamiuts of Alaska:

> Then he told of the great flood, when the water rose and rose. The Nunamiuts took refuge on the hill called Umiat, about a thousand feet high, by the Colville River. They were there for a long time, till at last the raven came to their help. It pierced a fragment of dry land with its spear, and the sea fell. The great sea beasts made their way out, and where they followed a tortuous course the rivers now run in zigzags.[64]

The constantly recurring raven theme (a vulture in the Mexican version) is remarkable in the extreme. What can account for such a universal correspondence unless it be a common source? Some might say that birds of carrion would naturally be associated with any disastrous flood, for they would be much in evidence consuming the corpses. But in that case the memory of them would be one of revulsion and not of appreciation. The Nunamiuts revere the raven.

The modern world is filled with debunkers—those whose chief delight is to explode some idea that trusting souls have long accepted. Among these ideas is that of the confirmation of the flood by archaeology. Many have energetically played this down. But after all due allowances are made for hyper-enthusiasm at the findings, the fact remains that many competent scholars are convinced the confirmation is real. Says Toynbee:

---

64. Helge Ingstadt, *Nunamiut,* p. 175.

It has remained for modern archaeologists to discover the original version of the legend and also to find direct evidence of a particular flood of abnormal severity in a thick layer of flood-laid clay which intervenes between the earliest and the later strata deposited by human habitation on the sites of certain historic seats of the Sumeric culture.[65]

Others concur:

In 1929 two archaeological parties, one at Ur and one at Kish, made a singular discovery. Having removed beds formed of pottery and debris, they found a layer of clay perfectly smooth and homogeneous. The workmen declared that the bed of the river had been reached, but continuing to dig, after four feet ten and one half inches of clay the archaeologists were surprising [sic] to find pottery reappearing more archaic and of a finer quality. . . . It seems scarcely possible that a deposit of four feet ten and one half inches of clay was formed by the rivers alone, even aided by exceptional rains.[66]

Eventually Woolley was able to show that the great flood of the Gilgamesh Epic and the Biblical deluge were identical, and that, moreover, the flood was an historic fact.[67]

But George Barton is convinced that the findings do not substantiate the Biblical flood:

. . . there is, in reality, no evidence that these deposits of silt mean more than that for a time the Euphrates and Tigris changed their beds and flowed for a time over parts of Ur and Kish that had previously been inhabited. . . . Henri Frankfort, indeed, has since shown that, from the evidence of the pottery found above and below the strata of silt on the two sites, the two inundations did not occur at the same time, and were not even in the same century! They could not then, have been the Biblical flood. There are evidences of a temporary submergence of the two sites by changes in the course of the rivers.[68]

---

65. Arnold Toynbee, *A Study of History,* p. 73.

66. Daniel-Rops, *Sacred History,* p. 68.

67. Ceram, *op. cit.,* p. 303.

68. Quoted by Merrill F. Unger, *Archaeology and the Old Testament,* p. 47.

With this quotation Dr. Unger disposes of the evidence. It could be wished he had given more evidence for rejecting Woolley's position. It does not seem likely that a river, on a temporary change of course, would leave a deposit of eight feet. It is also unlikely that a river should change its course in such a way as to inundate a city, not to say that two rivers should inundate two cities. And pottery dating is not an exact thing—in the so dim past the archaeologist does well to hit the right century. At any rate, we may say that in the opinion of many scholars of mature judgment the flood is confirmed by the excavations of Woolley at Ur, and of Langdon and Mackay at Kish.

The Book of Genesis clearly indicates that within the purview of history the race of man was originally one and of one language. Many have thought it beneath their scholarly acumen even to consider the possible historicity of such a statement. Yet some evidence is coming to light that the story of Babel and the confusion of tongues is real and historical. De Meiss-Teuffen, a sailor-of-fortune who has sailed small boats all over the globe, reports a tradition of the island of Madagascar:

In the beginning there were three brothers, fair of skin and beautiful, who divided the world among themselves. . . . The natives were afraid of the dark. They couldn't understand why there shouldn't be a full moon every night. At last they decided to build a great tower, trap the moon, and put it to work full time. Day by day it rose closer to the sky. All went well till a log fell off and killed a worker. His relatives said he'd been murdered and a fight ensued in which many men were killed. From that day forward, there was feuding between the tribes which caused them to separate; they lost the ability to speak the same language and comprehend each other.[69]

Notice the correspondences to the Biblical story:

(1) An absolute beginning postulated for humanity.
(2) Three brothers fathered the whole human race.

---

69. Hans De Meiss-Teuffen, *Wanderlust*, p. 131.

(3) Early men were all one race and one language.
(4) Building of a great tower was begun in objection to
    heavenly appointments.
(5) Dissension arose to disrupt the work.
(6) Men lost the ability to speak the same language.

It seems out of the question that there is no relation between
the two stories. As one anthropologist put it:

. . . such things as tobacco or the alphabet are known to have
spread from one source; we have their history, and their distribution is what you might expect. And therefore when a group of
similarities is found between the Paleo-Siberians and some of the
northwestern Indians, just across the Bering Sea from one
another, and including such things as a series of myths in which
the Raven is a major figure, the argument for diffusion is
irresistible.[70]

Dr. Howells is explicit on the matter of the original unity
of alphabetic language:

. . . by about 1200 B.C. somewhere in Phoenicia, a completely new
set of 22 signs was put to use for the same purpose, and this is
the alphabet from which came all those of history: ours, Hebrew,
Arabic, Hindu and others.[71]

If he is right, why is it so hard to receive the statement of
Genesis 11:1 that "the whole earth was of one language and
of one speech"?

There are remains of numbers of towers on the plains
of Mesopotamia, the best preserved of which is that of Ur.
But none could compare with the glory which was that of
the Tower of Babel. Today it is evidenced by a tremendous
hole in the ground used through the centuries as a quarry
for the removal of bricks for other construction purposes.
Herodotus describes eight superimposed terraces, in one of
the lower of which was a temple housing the statue of
Marduk composed of eight hundred talents of pure gold.

---

70. William Howells, *Back of History*, p. 265.
71. *Ibid.*, p. 327.

The Tower, 300 feet high, was adorned by this gold-plated temple and its bluish enameled brick. From the level plains of Babylon, this edifice must have been the first and most breathtaking sight to greet the traveler's eye; and once inside the city, he would soon learn that the Tower also dominated the religious, political, and social life of Babylon.

There are a number of records left by Babylonian rulers concerning the divine directions given them for building or rebuilding the Tower. Among them is that of Nabopolassar:

At that time Marduk commanded me to build the Tower of Babel, which had become weakened by time and fallen into disrepair; he commanded me to ground its base securely on the breast of the underworld, whereas its pinnacles should strain upwards to the skies.[72]

It is important to note that at Nabopolassar's time (seventh century B.C.) the Tower was already ancient.

The Biblical account is historical in the notice about the use of bitumen in the Tower's construction. In the tower at Ur the bricks are still very tightly held together by bitumen.

The Tower of Babel has arisen out of the mists of hoary antiquity to put to shame the faces of those who have said that the Bible story was a fabrication to explain the world's dissimilitude of languages.

Another Biblical reference which customarily has been taken with a benign smile by the modern mind concerns the longevity of the antediluvians. There is less inclination to smile now. In 2100 B.C. the Babylonians had chroniclers, who compiled catalogues of the then ancient antediluvian kings, together with those after the Flood, which latter are treated as entirely historical. The pre-Flood kings were counted in the tablets as being fabulously long-lived. Most modern scholars have long rejected any historicity for these king-lists. Woolley, however, has recently documented the existence of one of those appearing in the king-lists, Mas-anni-

---

72. Ceram, *op. cit.*, p. 288.

padda, the founder of the third dynasty after the Flood, whose name appears on a limestone foundation tablet at Ur. This historical confirmation of the lists makes it more likely that there is some historical basis for their assignment of extreme longevity to the antediluvian kings; and these in turn should cause us to hesitate to reject the Biblical statements. In addition, there are similar accounts of primitive longevity in Berosus, Babylonian historian of 300 B.C., and in the traditions of the Persians, Egyptians, Hindus, Greeks and others.

The modern mind, with its preoccupation with the theory of gradual progression, has long frowned upon the Biblical representation of fairly high culture among the earliest men.[73] Egyptology should have taught us better, though, for it has long spoken of an artistry reaching back millennia before the Christian era. Some of the Egyptian items which belie the early brutishness of men are—

(1) A painter's palette, about 3000 B.C.
(2) Dynastic beginnings at perhaps 3200.
(3) The pyramid of Cheops (2500), a monstrous tower 736 feet in the air. According to *The Encyclopaedia Britannica,* ". . . the brain power to which it testifies is as great as that of any modern man." [74]
(4) Burial vaults made so tight by the closeness of fit of the stones without mortar that "neither needle nor hair" can be inserted in the joints.[75]
(5) An amulet of pure iron from the mummy of Tutankhamen (*c.* 1350 B.C.).
(6) The golden effigy of King Tutankhamen thus described by Ceram:

The gold glittered as brightly as if it had just come from the foundry. The head and hands were cast in three dimensions, but the highly decorated remainder of the figure was rendered in low relief. Crossed hands held the royal emblems of Crook and Flail,

---

73. Genesis 4:16 ff.
74. Quoted by Halley, *op. cit.*, p. 91.
75. *Cf.* Ceram, *op. cit.*, p. 146.

inlaid with blue faience. The face was of pure gold, the eyes of lapis-lazuli glass. This bright visage had a rigid, masklike look, and yet seemed alive.[76]

The mask was inlaid with pieces of glass of many colors, lapis-lazuli, green feldspar, carnelian, alabaster, and obsidian.

The monuments of Egypt have long stood to bear witness to the culture of early man as indicated in the Scriptures. But now there is coming to light additional confirmation. Abraham is represented in Genesis 23 as weighing out four hundred shekels of silver which was "current with the merchant." This has long been held as an anachronism. It was supposed that it is impossible to think of men of 2000 B.C. having a definite system of weights and values; but recent discoveries at Ur, Abraham's home town, have shown that there was a vast system of commerce, involving all sorts of business transactions, radiating from Ur. In the nineteenth century scholars wrote many things about the Near East which have had to be revised or even rejected since better access to the facts has been gained through such studies as those of Woolley at Ur.

It was once the custom of scholars to date the Mosaic law code much later than the middle fifteenth century B.C. They said that any legal systems that compared favorably with modern jurisprudence must have a long development from primitive man. And in the fifteenth century B.C., as far as they knew, man was very primitive in Palestine. Now we know that there were well-systemized legal codes in existence as early as the twenty-first century B.C. in Mesopotamia.

And when, in 1947, the American archaeologist Francis Steele fitted together four cuneiform fragments found at Nippur, he found that he had discovered a section of the legal code of King Lipit-ishtar (2102–1092 B.C.).[77]

---

76. *Ibid.*, p. 197.
77. *Ibid.*, p. 304.

The code of Hammurabi, a magnificent system of justice, was distributed throughout the Babylonian kingdom in the twentieth century B.C. Why is it thought a thing incredible that a well-schooled Hebrew in the fifteenth century should have drawn up a fine system of law?

Men write today of the Stone Age or the Bronze Age as though in those times the whole world was peopled by wild-eyed denizens of the forest; but there is nothing about works in bronze that demands a brutishness in men; indeed, the very opposite is true. Today we are great users of bronze; and we consider it in better taste for works of culture than steel. Yet bronze-working was a highly developed art in the tenth century B.C. Solomon's ". . . copper refineries at Ezion-Geber used methods rediscovered less than a hundred years ago in the Bessemer process." [78] Ducts were provided to make use of a strong natural draft in the mountainous arrangement at Ezion-Geber. Now there are some indications that iron was known much earlier than commonly supposed. Witness the iron amuletic headrest of the mummy of Tutankhamen.[79] In this connection it is startling to note that according to some scholars the Hittites named the Perizzites from the Hittite word for iron—*parziili.*[80]

In view of the vast knowledge of ancient culture coming to light, there is no reason any more to deny the historicity of Biblical references to it. Why, Assurbanipal, himself now an ancient ruler, collected 30,000 volumes on the culture which was ancient when he was modern—volumes (clay tablets) dealing with most of the major fields of inquiry known to twentieth-century man!

One of the best vindications of an allegedly unhistorical narrative is that of Abraham and the Battle of Four Kings Against Five. Abraham is pictured in Genesis 14 as winning a victory with the help of his servants and allies over Ched-

78. Professor Nelson Glueck, quoted by T. Engelder, *The Scripture Cannot Be Broken,* p. 209.

79. *Cf.* Ceram, *op. cit.,* p. 201.

80. *Cf.* James Muir, *The Spade and the Scriptures,* p. 25.

orlaomer, king of Elam, Tidal king of Goiim, Amraphel king of Shinar and Arioch king of Ellasar. These had routed the Sodomite confederation in the vale of Siddim, where there were slime (bitumen) pits. Even today there is much bitumen in and around the Dead Sea.

Amraphel is commonly identified with Hammurabi, since phonetically the two words are almost the same. He ruled over Babylon a little later than the Biblical time given for Abraham. According to the Spartoli Tablets (2000–1800 B.C.) Babylon was overrun by Tudhula, Eri-Aku, and Kudur-Lahamal, among others. Tudhula is described, not as king of a town but simply "of nations" as in the Bible. These tablets tell us that Kudur-Lahamal was accompanied by a people called the Umman-Mandu, mercenary troops from various nations. Etymologically Ellasar could be "the city of Larsa," now called Senkereh. Shinar, of course, is the region that had Babylon for its center.

The fact that the invaders are represented as marching down from Haran and skirting the eastern edge of what is now Transjordania used to be regarded as final proof of the legendary character of the narrative. Now, however, an ancient route has been authenticated by numerous mounds along this line of march.

The Biblical date for the Exodus around 1441 B.C. fits very well into the general historical picture of that time. Amenhotep II was Pharaoh at this date. His father, Thutmose III, would be the Pharaoh of the Oppression, a role he was admirably suited to fill, according to the monumental records of his conquests and buildings. The monuments show him using Semitic slaves in his vast building projects. The taskmasters tell them, "The rod is in my hand; be not idle." [81] Amenhotep II succeeded him and carried out his oppressive measures. Amenhotep's successor was not his firstborn but a younger son, as the famous "Dream Inscription" at the base of the Sphinx indicates. Therein Thut-

---

81. Merrill F. Unger, *Archaeology and the Old Testament,* p. 143.

mose IV recounts how in a dream the sphinx appeared to him with the startling news that he would one day be king of Egypt. This indicates that the eldest brother met an untimely death; or else the law of primogeniture, in effect at that time in Egypt, would have made him ruler upon the death of his father. Thus the circumstance of the premature death of Pharaoh's firstborn is corroborated.

The invasion of Canaan by Israel is given a possible place in the historical perspective by the Tel-el-Amarna letters, written by the governors of Canaan to their Egyptian overlords, pleading for help against the marauding "Habiru," the phonetic equivalent of "Hebrew." The letters date around 1400, the Biblical date of the entrance into Canaan, about forty years after the Exodus.

(5) Vindication of the Mosaic Authorship of the Pentateuch

One of the sharpest contradictions of a Biblical statement by the modern mind concerns the authorship of the Pentateuch. Exodus, Leviticus, Numbers, and Deuteronomy very frequently (about 104 times scattered throughout the four books) claim that Moses was the human source of these records. The objection that what we now call "The Book of Genesis" nowhere claims Moses for its author is obviated by the fact that the Pentateuch was held from our earliest knowledge to be a unit. The book of Numbers begins with the word "and." In Deuteronomy 31:24–26, it is expressly claimed that Moses wrote ". . . the words of this law in a book, until they were finished . . ." and that he delivered them to the Levites to keep with the ark. The word "law" is the same as "Torah," the age-old Jewish designation for the first five books.

It may be said here that there is a decided swing in critical study back to respect for the claim of Mosaic authorship. Beginning in the eighteenth century, attention was focused on the variations in the divine names in the Pentateuch. Jean Astruc, a French physician, argued for two main source documents for Genesis, an Elohist and a Jehovist, but maintained the Mosaic authorship. Eichhorn, at first holding this position, later dismissed the Mosaic authorship. In the late nineteenth century, Wellhausen claimed that since the prophets knew nothing of a highly developed sacrificial system such as is indicated in Leviticus, such accounts must be post-exilic. Now the critics propose four principal sources which a post-exilic writer wove together to suit the purposes of a priestly reform: the Jehovist (J), the Elohist (E), the Deuteronomist (D), and the priestly school (P).

Professor Oswald T. Allis, in his monumental *The Five Books of Moses*, has adequately met the objections to the Mosaic authorship. He shows that Josephus, the claims of the Pentateuch, the testimony of the rest of the Bible, especially of Jesus, and the voice of tradition all affirm the Mosaic authorship. Some of the objections he meets are as follows:

"The difference in names proves the difference of source." He shows that often the variation is due to the intention of the writer to utilize the various names to emphasize various aspects of the divine character. Thus, "Elohim" emphasizes the power and creativity of God, whereas "Jehovah" calls to mind his redemptive purpose. This also answers the objection drawn from Exodus 6:3, which the critics say proves that the word "Jehovah" was unknown before the time of Moses. It is evident (they say) that since the name Jehovah is often found in Genesis as known to the patriarchs, Moses could not have written these narratives. But Dr. Allis points out that to "be known by the name Jehovah" did not signify mere acquaintance with the appellation, but much more deeply, according to Old Testament usage, to have personal experience of the redemptive character of God as was epitomized in the name Jehovah. Thus, Moses could use the name in writing of the patriarchal period, since the patriarchs were acquainted with the name but did not realize its significance, as set forth here, to Moses, and as taught by God's mighty acts in the deliverance of Israel.

"The choice of words is different in the various sections." Since the variations in diction under the theory of Mosaic authorship can be paralleled in the works of most of the great English writers, the argument from diction is of very little force.

"Double narratives betray composite authorship." The Pentateuchal instances where an account is given twice is in no way inimical to the theory of Mosaic authorship. Allis has shown that it is characteristic of Hebrew literature to give a summary statement first, and then to begin anew and give a detailed account, as in the creation records. One striking point Allis has made is that the critical theory would break up many of the manifest poetical units which the critics accept.

"The sacrificial system is post-exilic." This brings us to the principal contention of the fragmentizing critics, namely that the sacrificial system of the Pentateuch was unknown to the prophets. For proof they usually point to Jeremiah 7:22 ff. Here Jehovah says: "For I spake not unto your fathers, nor commanded them in the day I brought them out of the land of Egypt, concerning burnt offerings or sacrifices. . . ." However, the word rendered "concerning" here is not the equivalent of our common "about" or "concerning." While this rare word may sometimes mean "about" or "concerning," it usually has a stronger meaning such as "because of" or "for the sake of." Hence, in the verse under question, a natural rendering would be: "I spake not unto your fathers nor commanded them in the day that I brought them out of Egypt, for the sake of burnt offerings or sacrifices . . ."—that is, Jehovah did not ordain the sacrificial system because he needed the food of the burnt offering nor as a religious end in itself, but as a means to the attainment of a righteous life (see verse 23). If the people persist in begrudging the surrender of the meat in the burnt offering, let them go ahead and eat it as they do in the sacrifices. The sacrifice offerings could be eaten lawfully after they were offered; the burnt offering was to be entirely consumed by fire. The people, viewing the offerings as a religious end in themselves, were wishing that they might also eat the flesh of the burnt offerings. Jehovah says that if they are missing the spiritual lesson in the regulations, they may as well disregard them. The burnt offering was supposed to be an overt expression of one's entire committal to Jehovah. Allis shows that the prophets were not speaking against the sacrificial system *per se,* but against a mechanical application of it. Compare Jeremiah 17:21 ff., where the prophet commends both Sabbath observance and the ideal offering of sacrifices together with "sacrifices of praise." The prophets endorse sacrifice when the heart is in it.

This interpretation is one that is in keeping with good linguistic requirements and with the bulk of the literature which preceeds Jeremiah. The critical interpretation requires the vast pre-exilic priestly literature to be displaced from its age-old accepted chronological position. Rather, this is a verse critics have found as a justification for such displacement. But for such a radical step one should have references that admit of no easy other explanation.

(6) Evidence of Early Well-developed Ideas

One of the commonest arguments against the authenticity of Biblical records is that they represent certain noble ideas as being very early. The modern mind, operating from its theory of the gradual natural development of things, insists that the presence of well-developed ideas is proof of lateness. Thus, the tendency is to give a late date to the lofty passages in the Pentateuch or the Gospels. It is the contention of form criticism that the material in the Gospels is "traditional" and was not written down until some generations after the events which inspired them. Hence, we may only guess what those events originally were, or what were the words originally spoken. Now, the word "traditional" is ambiguous. In II Thessalonians, Paul speaks of the gospel as the tradition; but his usage is poles away from that of the form critics. With him, "the tradition" is that doctrine which is delivered *(paradosis)* by an apostle directly to those who believed it, "whether by word or by epistle." With the form critics it is something passed along for generations. These critics postulate that the ideas of the Gospels are so refined that they must have a long development behind them.

The recently discovered Dead Sea Scrolls refute this position. They show that many of the ideas of the Gospels were already written down in refined form before the first century. The very manner of their discovery supports the story Jesus told of the lost sheep, for the Bedouin who found the cave of the MSS did so while looking for a lost sheep in the Judaean Wilderness in 1947. The scrolls are called Ain-Feshka after the near-by stream and include a complete MS of Isaiah, a commentary on Habakkuk, a manual of discipline for the community of the New Covenant (all in Hebrew), and an Apocalypse of Lamech (Aramaic). According to one very capable scholar "the latest possible date" for the scrolls is A.D. 66–70.[82] Yet in them are written down some ideas in a form that the form critics have been saying must be generations later. Here is a list of them.

The synoptic accounts of the Sermon on the Mount refer to the blessing of the poor (in heart). *The Psalm of Thanksgiving* in the Dead Sea Scrolls says: "Thou hast redeemed the soul of the poor . . ."—described by Dupont-Sommer as "the one faithful to the New Covenant." [83]

The Gospel of Luke refers to the "New Covenant in my blood which is poured out for you," Jesus evidently viewing the shedding of his blood as a gift on behalf of men.[84] *The*

---

82. A. Dupont-Sommer, *The Dead Sea Scrolls,* p. 71.
83. *Ibid.*
84. Luke 22:20.

Rule of the New Covenant (Dead Sea Scrolls) speaks of "the Covenant of Grace." [85] In the Damascus Document it is called "the New Covenant." [86]

In the Gospels the idea is presented that Jesus is Deity. In the *Habakkuk Commentary* "the Master of Justice" is described in words reserved by the Jews for the appearance of Jehovah himself.[87]

The *Habakkuk Commentary* asserts the resurrection of "the Master of Justice," as the Gospels do for their Master.

The Gospels everywhere speak of faith in Jesus as the prerequisite to justification with God.[88] In the *Habakkuk Commentary* faith in "the Master of Justice" is the faith which saves.[89]

The suffering and tragic end of Messiah occupies about one-fourth of the total Gospel narratives. The same theme is a dominant one in the *Habakkuk Commentary*, according to Dupont-Sommer.[90]

The *Habakkuk Commentary* has a well-developed eschatology that has several striking correspondences with the little apocalypses of the Synoptics and with the Johannine accounts. There was to be a "last generation," "a final time" known only to God, much violence and treachery and unbelief "at the end of the days," a time of chastisement on the wicked of Israel and the Gentiles and on Jerusalem, and a glorious return of the Master to be awaited.[91]

With regard to the *Testaments of the Twelve Patriarchs*, Dupont-Sommer is convinced of the error of calling perplexing Christological texts later interpolations.

. . . these "Christological" passages taken as a whole, henceforth seem to be of the greatest worth, and to continue to reject them

---

85. Dupont-Sommer, *op. cit.*, p. 46.
86. *Ibid.*, p. 64.
87. *Ibid.*, p. 44.
88. *Cf.* John 8:24, 20:31, Luke 24:46–47, and the various commissions.
89. Dupont-Sommer, *op. cit.*, p. 44.
90. *Ibid.*, p. 34.
91. *Ibid.*, pp. 41 ff.

a priori as being of Christian origin would appear to be contrary to all sound method. It is now certain—and this is one of the most important revelations of the Dead Sea discoveries—that Judaism of the first century B.C. saw a whole theology of the suffering Messiah, of a Messiah who should be the redeemer of the world, developing around the person of the Master of Justice.[92]

Thus the Dead Sea Scrolls have shown that ideas similar to those recorded in the New Testament were positively in written existence by the time of the first century A.D. To say the least, this seriously undermines the position of those who reject the authenticity of the Gospels and other New Testament writings on the grounds that such ideas could not have been in existence so early. As Dupont-Sommer has concluded, "since the historical milieu is better known, Jesus and the nascent Christian Church will find themselves more firmly rooted in history."[93]

(7) Vindication of the Book of Isaiah

Today one runs the risk of being called obscurantist if he suggests that Isaiah wrote the whole book attributed to him in the canon. Most students suppose that chapters 40–66 were written by an anonymous exilic prophet or prophets, chapters 40–55 when Cyrus was already on the horizon as a powerful challenger to the supremacy of Babylon, and chapters 56–66 after the return to Palestine. This position more seriously affects the question of Biblical inspiration than might at first be supposed. The whole section turns on the claim of the prophet that Jehovah's true deity is proved by his ability to predict distant future events accurately. Compare the following statements to this effect:

Who hath wrought and done it, calling the generations from the beginning? I, Jehovah, the first and with the last, I am he. (41:4)

---

92. *Ibid.*, pp. 95–96.
93. *Ibid.*, p. 100.

Produce your cause, saith Jehovah, bring forth your strong reasons, saith the King of Jacob. Let them bring forth and declare unto us what shall happen: declare ye the former things, what they are, that we may consider them, and know the latter end of them; or show us things to come. Declare the things that are to come hereafter, that we may know that ye are gods: yea, do good, or do evil, that we may be dismayed, and behold it together. (41:21–23)

Who hath declared it from the beginning, that we may know? and beforetime, that we may say, He is right? yea, there is none that declareth, yea, there is none that showeth, yea, there is none that heareth your words. (41:26)

Behold, the former things are come to pass, and new things do I declare; before they spring forth I tell you of them. (42:9)

And who, as I, shall call, and shall declare it, and set it in order for me, since I established the ancient people? and the things that are coming, and that shall come to pass, let them declare. (44:7)

. . . that confirmeth the word of his servant, and performeth the counsel of his messengers; that saith of Jerusalem, She shall be inhabited; and of the cities of Judah, They shall be built, and I will raise up the waste places thereof; that saith to the deep, Be dry, and I will dry up thy rivers; that saith of Cyrus, He is my shepherd, and shall perform all my pleasure, even saying of Jerusalem, She shall be built, and of the temple, Thy foundation shall be laid. (44:26–28)

I am Jehovah, and there is none else; besides me there is no God. I will gird thee, though thou hast not known me; that they may know from the rising of the sun, and from the west, that there is none besides me: I am Jehovah, and there is none else. (45:5–6)

Thus saith Jehovah, the Holy One of Israel, and his Maker: Ask me of the things that are to come; concerning my sons, and concerning the work of my hands, command ye me. (45:11)

Remember the former things of old: for I am God, and there is none else; I am God, and there is none like me; declaring the end from the beginning, and from ancient times things that are not yet done; saying, My counsel shall stand, and I will do all my pleasure; calling a ravenous bird from the east, the man of my counsel from a far country; yea, I have spoken, I will also bring it to pass; I have purposed, I will also do it. (46:9–11)

Because I knew that thou are obstinate, and thy neck is an iron sinew, and thy brow brass; therefore I have declared it to thee from of old; before it came to pass I showed it thee; lest thou shouldest say, Mine idol hath done them, and my graven image, and my molten image, hath commanded them. Thou hast heard it; behold all this; and ye, will ye not declare it? I have showed thee new things from this time, even hidden things, which thou hast not known. They are created now, and not from of old; and before this day thou heardest them not; lest thou shouldest say, Behold, I knew them. (48:4–7)

Repeatedly the writer presents his predictions of the conquests of Cyrus as proof of Jehovah's deity. It makes his claims a farce to place him in the exilic period when the events "predicted" were already imminent or even past! The whole argument from chapter 40 onward is based on the claim that Jehovah is revealing "things to come" of such a nature that when they are come to pass no one can say "Behold, I knew them."

The objections to the Isaianic authorship meet with more powerful objections than themselves. Let us consider the objections to the theory that a contemporary of Cyrus composed chapters 40–66, called the Deutero-Isaiah theory.

(1) If the author wrote on the eve of the fall of Babylon to Cyrus, as the critics claim, why does Deutero-Isaiah accuse Babylon of being genuinely confident of her own security?

Now therefore hear this, thou that are given to pleasures, that sittest securely, that sayest in thy heart, I am, and there is none else besides me; I shall not sit as a widow, neither shall I know the loss of children: but these two things shall come to thee in a moment in one day, the loss of children, and widowhood; in their full measure shall they come upon thee, in the multitude of thy sorceries, and the great abundance of thine enchantments. For thou hast trusted in thy wickedness; thou hast said, None seeth me; thy wisdom and thy knowledge, it hath perverted thee; and thou hast said in thy heart, I am, and there is none else beside me. Therefore shall evil come upon thee; thou shalt not know the dawning thereof: and mischief shall fall upon thee; thou shalt not be able to put it away: and desolation shall come upon thee suddenly, which thou knowest not.[94]

Notice that the prophet's warning is of an *unexpected* doom. The evil falls upon them "suddenly"—the Babylonians do "not know the dawning thereof." But according to the Deutero-Isaiah theory, Cyrus had already defeated Croesus, overrun Lydia, and taken Croesus' gold. George Adam Smith says:

Unless he had already appeared in flesh and blood, and was on the point of striking at Babylon, with all the prestige of unbroken victory, a great part of Isa. xli–xlviii would be utterly unintelligible.[95]

King tells us that the priests of that country were disaffected under the rulership of Nabonidus, in whose reign Babylon fell.[96] This same authority speaks of the "unsatisfactory condition of the Babylonian army during Nebuchadnezzar's closing years." [97] Cyrus' easy investment of Babylon was in large measure due to the general and well-known discontent of the people, priesthood, city officials, and army officers under the existing misrule. Surely Nabonidus and Belshazzar were not unaware of all this. Yet a well-informed Hebrew prophet in the midst of it all says that Babylon is one that is oblivious to any threat to her dominion, "that sittest securely, that sayest *in thine heart,* I am, and there is none besides me." Opponents of the Deutero-Isaiah theory may say that this can be better explained as Isaiah's forecast of the rise of Babylon to world dominion. As he looked at the whole range of Babylon's future history, before she was even a world power, he focused his prophecy on the pride and arrogance with which Nebuchadnezzar would deal with Jehovah's

94. Isaiah 47:8–11.
95. G. A. Smith, *The Book of Isaiah,* Vol. 2, p. 9.
96. L. W. King, *History of Babylon,* p. 284.
97. *Ibid.,* p. 281.

chosen people, and on her subsequent swift decline under his immediate successors.[98]

The case for the Isaianic authorship is well-stated by Dr. Francisco:

The passages in dispute are, in the Old Testament canon, a part of the Book of Isaiah. There is no indication that another writer is the author. No name appears in all the book except that of the son of Amoz. It is difficult to see how another book could have been added to that of Isaiah. If it has happened, it is strange that the author's name is unknown. "Inferior men who wrote at the same time have been remembered, but the greatest prophet Judah ever produced has been absolutely forgotten—so absolutely, that not a whisper concerning him comes down to us from the past." There would be reason for concealing his name before the fall of Babylon, but not afterwards. "Further, how could the home-coming exiles, in whose hearts his words must have stood uppermost of all prophecies, forget his name?"[99]

In reply he says: "These arguments are the most difficult of all to answer, for nothing but conjecture can be used."[100] His explanation of the anonymity of the prophet is as follows: "The absence of the prophet's name in Jewish history remains an enigma. It may be that, wishing his people to follow his word rather than his person, he preferred to be but a 'voice crying in the wilderness.'"[101]

This brings us to the second objection:

(2) How can we so inadequately explain Deutero-Isaiah's anonymity[102] and yet hold confidently to it? During the exile the Jews were deprived of ceremonial worship; and this was compensated for by scribal activity and the reading of sacred

---

98. *Cf.* Isaiah 39:6.

99. C. T. Francisco, Thesis: *The Authorship and Unity of Isaiah 40–66*, p. 85.

100. *Ibid.*, pp. 85–86.

101. *Ibid.*, p. 87.

102. Franz Delitzch says, "It will always remain a mystery." *Isaiah*, Vol. 2, Fourth Edition, p. 133.

literature. The history that we have strongly suggests that there is unbroken scribal activity from the time of the exile till the time of the writing of the *Wisdom of Sirach* and the translation of the Septuagint.

546 Approximate beginning of Deutero-Isaiah's literary activity, according to Francisco.[103]
538 Return under Zerubbabel.
515 Completion of second temple.
474 Esther and Mordecai, and intense national spirit of the Jews.
458 Second great return, under Ezra.
445 Nehemiah comes to Jerusalem.
433 Levites re-established in Jerusalem.
350 Jaddua high priest.
332 Alexander the Great at temple, pays respect to the prophetical writings.
300 Simon the Great, high priest.
250 Jesus ben Sirach attributes this section to Isaiah.
200 LXX translation of the Prophets made.
100 Date Albright prefers for newly discovered complete roll of Isaiah at Ain-Feshka.

The seventy top-flight Jerusalem scholars who made the Septuagint translation give no indication of suspicion of a Deutero-Isaiah. Jesus ben Sirach, in the *Wisdom of Sirach,* affirms the Isaianic authorship. Throughout the interval between Deutero-Isaiah's literary activity and these two literary productions there was continuously a body of professional law-keepers whose very heart and soul was the study of the sacred literature. Yet, according to the said theory, somewhere within this time one or more of them "accidently or erroneously" added Deutero-Isaiah's roll to that of Isaiah; and when they had done so, all the others and all the people and all the historians fell in with their error.

Suppose, for a moment, that Deutero-Isaiah's roll was anonymous, and as such came into the hands of the body of

---

103. Francisco, *op. cit.,* p. 190.

scribes, and these scribes understood its exilic origin. At least for many years afterwards the interpretation of it in religious instruction would be as of unquestioned exilic origin. But according to our theory, somewhere in the period of time I have sketched above, there was a complete revolution in interpretation, and not one voice was raised in protest—a thing unparalleled in all interpretational history, not to say, Jewish interpretational history.

(3) If Deutero-Isaiah ridiculed the exiles about idol-worship, did he not rub salt into open wounds? According to the analogy of prophecy, we may ascertain some things a prophet would not do. No other prophet dwells reproachfully on an offense of which the offender is already ashamed and for which he has already received punishment. And why does he omit the most overwhelming argument of all— namely, that the exiles' idols had been powerless to save them from captivity and had themselves gone into captivity? Isaiah 46:1 speaks of Babylonish idols themselves going into captivity. "Bel boweth down, Nebo stoopeth; their idols are upon the beasts, and upon the cattle: the things that ye carried about are made a load, a burden to the weary beast." But no mention is made of the Hebrew idols having already suffered such a fate. If Deutero-Isaiah was speaking to the exiles, would not the captivity of their own idols have been the most conclusive argument against them? The passage makes better sense if we understand the prophet to be deriding the idolatry of the Babylon which would fall, speaking with a view to being heard by the idolatrous Israelites of his own day.

(4) There *is* such a thing as prophetic perfect; but where else in all the Bible does a prophet speak of a past event as though future? When the author read Isaiah 43:38, "Therefore I *will profane* the princes of the sanctuary; and I *will make* Jacob a curse, and Israel a reviling," he said to himself, "How does George Adam Smith reconcile that to the exilic authorship?" Turning to his translation, the author found that he had put it in the past, footnoting: "So from

signs in the LXX, Klostermann, Cheyne, Whitehouse, Box. Heb., I will profane the princes of the Sanctuary." [104]

(5) If Isaiah predicted subservience to Assyria, miraculous deliverance from Assyria, the fall to Babylon, the exile, the fall of Babylon to the Medes and Elamites (Persians), and the return of the Hebrew captives in chapters 1–39, why should it be thought a thing incredible that in chapters 40–66 he should go one step further and name and describe the victorious *king* of the Medes? To name Cyrus one hundred and fifty years ahead of time does not violate the analogy or prophecy any more than to name the country he would lead to power. Isaiah prophesied the speedy overthrow of Pekah and Rezin, and was vindicated in the eyes of all Israel. He prophesied the destruction of Sennacherib, and was vindicated. The people learned by this time that what Isaiah said would happen would happen. Then he scourged the people for their unjust way of life, and prophesied the Babylonian captivity. Even the king believed him. There were a few who already loved Jehovah, and a few more who repented and turned to him. But what hope was there for them? It is hard for us to realize what the thought of the destruction of Jerusalem meant to the truly religious Jew of Isaiah's day. Not willing to leave his spiritual kindred in despair, Isaiah outlined God's plan for the future with a certainty of tone and a confident attention to detail that could come only from God himself. These were no vague Sibylline oracles. God would send a deliverer, and his name was Cyrus, and they could look for restoration with a definiteness that gave stability to the soul. There is a close parallel in the New Testament. A time of unprecedented wickedness and oppression is predicted. But assurance is given that the saints in that day will be delivered from that time of terrible trouble by the coming of a Deliverer; and his name is given—it is Jesus. Reports are coming from Germany that it is this hope that is producing the most energetic revival

---

104. G. A. Smith, *The Book of Isaiah*, Vol. 2, p. 164.

of religion in that war-weary country. This promise is a boundless source of hope to many Christians in every time of deep distress. The oracles of the coming of Cyrus would have been a great hope to the otherwise discouraged exiles. Who can tell whether a substantial remnant of the faithful would have survived the captivity without these promises?

(6) Do slavish imitation and literary genius go together? Francisco gives the following likenesses between the first and second Isaiahs.[105]

> reduplication
> epanaphora
> crowding together of short sentences
> use of same words and phrases:
>> forty words in common beginning with aleph
>> "the Holy One of Israel"
>> "the Holy One"
>> "the Mighty One"
>> "saith Jehovah"
>> "the mouth of Jehovah hath spoken it"
>> "King" (as applied to God)
>> "streams of water"
>> "light"
>> "glow" or "fire"
>> "offspring"
>> "to dry up"
>> "my mountain"
>> "high and exalted"
>> "vexatious calamities"
>> "to call" (symbolically)

Nowhere outside Biblical literature do we find such a literally copying style to manifest such a great poet.

(7) Have we put the proper evaluation on the argument from style and theology?

Much has been made of the fact that, in spite of the

---

105. Francisco, *op. cit.*, pp. 105–10.

above-mentioned similarities, there are a number of significant expressions in 1–39 not in 40–66, and vice versa. Let us
apply this same test to the book of Ezekiel, which is generally considered authentic except by a few very recent radical
critics. There are forty-eight chapters. Let us test the second
half against the first half, or, if you prefer, Deutero-Ezekiel
against Ezekiel. Redpath provides us with an excellent list
of key phrases with their locations.[106] "Rebellious house"
occurs twelve times in the first twenty-four chapters and
none in the second twenty-four. "Execute judgments in the
midst of thee" is found five times in Ezekiel, and none in
Deutero-Ezekiel. The ratio is 8 to 0 in favor of Ezekiel for
"as I live, saith the Lord God," and 6 to 0 with respect to
"neither shall mine eye spare, and I also will have no pity,"
and 5 to 0 for Ezekiel with respect to "accomplish anger."
On the other hand Deutero-Ezekiel uses "the nether parts
of the earth" six times, as against none for Ezekiel. He uses
"in the land of the living" seven times, while it is not found
in the first half. The ratio in favor of the Second Ezekiel
is 4 to 0 with respect to "the terrible of the nations," and
7 to 0 with "the separate place." Is all this a weighty argument for Deutero-Ezekiel?

In the Gettysburg Address there are thirty-two significant expressions in the first half not in the latter half, and
twenty-three in the latter half not in the first half.

Some make large use of the different meanings of *tsedhek*
in the two sections of Isaiah to argue for Deutero-Isaiah. Its
root meaning seems to have been "either straightness, or
more probably soundness—the state in which a thing is all
right."[107] "In Arabic the cognate word is applied to a lance,
but this may mean a sound or fit lance as well as a straight
one."[108] It is easy to apply this "soundness" to soundness of
moral action, on the one hand, or to accuracy of statement

---

106. H. A. Redpath, *Ezekiel*, p. xvii.
107. Smith, *op. cit.*, p. 236.
108. *Ibid.*

on the other. Brown, Driver, and Briggs are most clear in giving the two meanings of the word: "rightness," "righteousness." [109] We ought to allow a great Hebrew prophet both uses of the word. Even a ruffian may say in one moment, "That guy was 'right,'" and later on, "He's a 'right' guy," using each of Isaiah's meanings.

There are many other lines of argument that could be pursued with regard to the authorship of Isaiah 40–66. Suffice it to say that to hold both its exilic authorship and its unity is a position comparable to No Man's Land. Most of the scholars have forsaken that position, denying the substantial unity of authorship of 40–66, of whom are B. Duhm, K. Littmann, A. Zillessen, G. E. Box, H. Odelberg, E. Sellin, T. K. Cheyne, W. H. A. Kosters, K. Budde, R. Abramowski, P. Volz, K. Marti, B. Stade, R. H. Kennett, S. Mowinckel, J. Skinner, Ewald, W. O. E. Oesterly, Franz Delitzch, G. A. Smith, and many others. It is either one or many Isaiahs. Are we prepared to follow the scholars into "the pervasive jungle of editorial matter in which all genuine prophecies are now hidden"? [110] Must we accept the conclusions that the majority of scholars come out with? If we let the prevailing scholarly opinion sway us, we must accept the more-than-dual authorship; but that is neither necessary nor desirable. There are some excellent scholars who maintain the essential unity of the book. Compare especially *The Unity of Isaiah,* by Oswald T. Allis. Whenever a cardinal doctrine like the authority of the Scriptures is called in question, it is our duty as Christians to go into the matter and decide for ourselves. The wonder-consciousness of the ancient oriental mind is abundantly evidenced in both Biblical and non-Biblical literature. The author of 40–66 is using two of Jehovah's wonders to show his true deity—two wonders that other gods cannot do, namely (1) give a reasonable

109. Brown, Driver, and Briggs, *A Hebrew and English Lexicon of the Old Testament,* p. 841.

110. R. H. Pfeiffer, *Introduction to the Old Testament,* p. 438.

explanation of how the universe started *(roshenoth,* "head-things") and (2) predict future events so far in advance as to exclude human prognostication. The writer's arguments are addressed to the whole Babylonian world. He says Jehovah it is who is calling, anointing, equipping, empowering (imperfects) Cyrus. If Cyrus is already on the scene and is already just about to invest Babylon itself, such a claim would be a mere assertion that could be matched by a prophet of Baal or of Marduk. But if it is a statement made more than a hundred years before it comes to pass, its divine origin cannot be questioned.

A CONSTRUCTIVE VIEW.—The Isaianic theory seems to furnish the most consistent framework for preserving the continuity and unity of the whole book. Those theories that insist on an actual historical setting throughout cause one to get the impression of being jerked back and forth in time and space.

If Isaiah in prophetic vision saw vividly before his eyes the Hebrew captives as they stumbled along the long road to Babylon, leaving behind a ruined temple, a smoking Jerusalem, why should he not be moved with compassion upon them? Why should he not want to speak words of reassurance to them, if he were aware of a factual basis for such words? Great preachers today speak passionately into a microphone to thousands they do not see; some are won to faith in Christ through this radio ministry. Usually, in such preaching, there is an audience that is present in addition to the unseen audience out beyond; the preacher sees this larger audience only by spiritual vision. So it is with Isaiah. With the broad sweep of providential history before him, he may draw forth ominous warnings to startle those of his immediate audience (his own generation) out of their complacent plunge into spiritual darkness; again, he may pronounce awful judgment on the proud and self-confident Babylonia of Nebuchadnezzar; again, he may speak words of comfort and reassurance to the pathetic exiles.

The analogy of prophecy[111] can be pushed to an unwarrantable extreme. The argument breaks down at certain points. Compare Abraham's vision of Israel's Egyptian bondage of 480 years; the prophecy about Josiah's defiling the heathen sanctuary; Isaiah's prophecy of the Babylonian sack of Jerusalem; the various messianic details; Jacob's prophecies of his sons' descendants; etc., etc. These were not more directly concerned with the contemporary scene than the prophecies of Isaiah 40–66. They served as assurance of God's control of human history and encouragement of success to those who aligned themselves with God's purposes.

(8) Vindication of the Book of Daniel

The prevailing scholarly view of the book of Daniel is that it is not a product of the man for whom it is named but of a Jew who wrote it around 167 B.C. to encourage revolt against the oppressive Antiochus Epiphanes.[112] For this position the following arguments are cited:

(1) The accuracy of the writer's statements about Maccabean times betrays that the writer was then living.
(2) The book contains many inaccuracies as to the days of the Babylonian ascendancy.
(3) The language is late. The presence of Aramaic and Greek words indicates a late date.

As to the first objection nothing can be answered except that the book claims to be supernaturally prophetic of the Grecian and post-Grecian era in the East. The *a priori* objection assumes that there cannot be detailed prediction of distant events—to overthrow a position held for centuries one needs more than *a priori* grounds.

---

111. The argument that Isaiah could not have authored the disputed passages since the case of a prophet's predicting distant events without primary meaning for his own generation has no parallel in other parts of scripture.

112. This view was first set forth by Porphyry of Tyre (born *c.* A.D. 232), an early outspoken opponent of Christianity.

One alleged historical inaccuracy concerns the treatment given Daniel by his Babylonian captors. The picture of such consideration as to give these foreign captives fine food and opportunity for learning is unrealistic against the background of the known cruelty of the Babylonians. Yet a great marble palace has been unearthed among the ruins of Babylon bearing the designation "The Place of Learning," where captive nobles were instructed in the wisdom of Chaldea.[113] This is not the first time that critics have disallowed the truth of a Biblical statement because of their own fragmentary knowledge of ancient history. It ill-behooves any scholar to say that a certain event could not have happened in a period of history of which the scholar does not have a fairly comprehensive knowledge. Yet most of the allegations of the anti-Biblicists are made in this way.

Another objection to the book's historicity used to be that Belshazzar was fictional—he was unknown to modern historians. He is no longer so. According to the partial knowledge of modern historians, Nabonidus was the last king of Babylon; and nothing was known of a Belshazzar. Now it has been established that Belshazzar was co-regent with Nabonidus. An inscription has been found in which an approximately equal respect is shown to each. The prayer cylinder of Nabonidus asks Bel to protect and prosper his son, Belshazzar. This knowledge helps to clear up an apparent contradiction in other inscriptions. In one, Gobryas claims, "In the night that I captured Babylon, I slew the king." Cyrus, however, in his annals relates: "In the day that I entered Babylon, I made the king my captive." Both statements are accurate. The two warriors are speaking of two different kings. Gobryas (perhaps the Darius of the Bible, who was Cyrus' chief general) slew Belshazzar, the king regent; and Cyrus, entering the city a little later, made captive Nabonidus, the titular king, who had hastily come up with his army in a vain attempt to ward off the invaders.

---

113. Harry Rimmer, *Dead Men Tell Tales*, p. 322.

When Nabonidus saw the city already invested, he surrendered to Cyrus.

Thus, in the very place where the book of Daniel was berated most, it is found to make its most valuable contribution to ancient history in describing the closing episode in the reign of the last acting ruler of Babylon. This is a great triumph for a book whose primary purpose is religious!

It is now known that the presence of Aramaisms in Biblical literature does not necessarily indicate a late date.

An Aramaic letter from King Adon of Ascalon, written to Pharaoh-necho of Egypt about 600 B.C. demonstrates that Aramaic had become the *lingua franca* of Palestine before the Chaldean conquest, as implied in II Kings 18:26. In addition to this, there are numerous recent finds of Aramaic papyri of the late fifth and sixth centuries B.C. published by G. R. Driver as well as a number of papyri from Elephantine in the Brooklyn Museum, published by E. G. Kraeling.[114]

The presence of Greek words in the book is not proof of late date, since Homer was writing refined Greek in the ninth century B.C. The spirit of the times was one of progress and international interest. It did not take long for ideas to pass from one people to another. Witness the case of Assurbanipal, who engraved on his monuments the likeness of a seven-stringed harp which was invented by the Greek poet Terpander just twenty-five years before the Assyrian's death.

Other evidences of the historicity of the book are available to the inquiring mind: extra-Biblical accounts of Nebuchadnezzar's madness, and in Babylon a den where beasts devoured political offenders, and a furnace inscribed: "This is the place of burning where men who blasphemed the gods of Chaldea died by fire." [115]

The fact that the book of Daniel has proved to be historical when most of its scholarly critics were certain it could

---

114. Merrill F. Unger, *Archaeology and the Old Testament*, p. 316.
115. *Cf.* Josephus, *Contra Apionem*, 1:20; Eusebius; Rimmer, *op. cit.*, p. 331.

not be is in itself evidence that there must be some other-than-natural explanation for its existence.

(9) Conclusion

It is not intended that this list of refuted historical criticisms is complete; nor need it be. It is enough to show that of the long list of objections by those who disavow the supernatural, those scholars who allow the supernatural have in scores of cases found conclusive evidence that the objections dissolve as we learn more of conditions in ancient times.[116] Of course, research has not yet told us everything it can of ancient history; but what it has told us has to a remarkable degree confirmed the Bible history and refuted those who objected to it. We know that life in the ancient empires was a complex thing. Many apparent contradictions were cleared up when we came to understand more of the complex situation. Time and again the Bible writers have located their narratives down in the midst of the intricacies of the times like a piece in a jigsaw puzzle and have done it right. It is amazing almost to the point of forceable recognition of the supernatural that this has been so often the case.

---

116. Th. Engelder, *op. cit.*, lists scores of criticisms which have been refuted.

CHAPTER V ❧ *The Bible offers the only satisfactory explanation of origins.*

A SATISFYING ACCOUNT OF ORIGINS

MEN ARE incurably curious as to the beginnings of things. To the question "What is the origin of all this wonderful universe," the Bible replies thus:

1. At some time in the indefinite past Yahweh God created the matter of the universe (Gen. 1:1).
2. At first the earth was unfit for habitation (Gen. 1:2).
3. God caused light to shine on the earth (Gen. 1:3).
4. This marked the completion of the first stage in God's development of the unorganized earth (Gen. 1:5).
5. Next, God caused a well-defined atmosphere (Heb., "expanse") to form, separating the water so that some was above it and some was below it (Gen. 1:6–7).
7. Next, God caused dry land to appear and to form the waters into seas. He caused the earth to produce various types of vegetation, each with seeds to reproduce its own form (Gen. 1:9–12).
8. This marked the completion of the third stage (Gen. 1:13).
9. Then God caused the sun, the moon and the other heavenly luminaries to shine on the earth (Gen. 1:14–18).
10. This constituted the fourth stage (Gen. 1:19).
11. God caused the waters to swarm (Heb.) with moving living things, including sea-monsters, and the air to be traversed by birds (Gen. 1:20–22).
12. This constituted the fifth stage (Gen. 1:23).
13. God caused the earth to send forth various animals each with a definite type of its own (Gen. 1:24–25).
14. God made man in a radically different and intimate way, in his own image, that is, with capacity for logical reflection, ethical distinction, and self-determination. He made him as the chief end of God's creation. He designed him for mastery

over the animate and inanimate world. (Gen. 1:26–30).
15. This constituted the sixth stage of God's development of the earth (Gen. 1:31).
16. It is implied that this marked the completion of God's development of the material universe, except as man should further develop it (Gen. 2:1–3; *cf*. Gen. 1:28).

This majestic survey of the origin of the earth carries with it the ring of authority. No other explanation has approached it for inherent consistency and grandeur, or for consonance with facts as they are progressively discovered. Many sciences, apart from the evolutionary bias of some of their investigators, have served to corroborate and amplify this Biblical account; but none has given so comprehensive or certain a picture. Compare W. F. Albright's words:

The account of Creation is unique in ancient literature. It undoubtedly reflects an advance monotheistic point of view, with a sequence of creative phases so rational that modern science cannot improve on it, given the same language and the same range of ideas in which to state its conclusions. In fact, modern scientific cosmogonies show a disconcerting tendency to be short lived and it may be seriously doubted whether science has yet caught up with the Biblical story.[1]

Ancient non-Biblical cosmogonies are for the most part absurd, such as the Egyptian idea of people emerging from the white worms left by the overflow of the Nile. The only serious modern rival to the Biblical explanation is the theory of biological evolution, which has projected itself into several other scientific fields so that many modern minds have felt that, by taking the evolutionary interpretation of the facts of biology and of geology and of anthropology, one could arrive at a reasonable explanation of the origin of things. Further investigation, however, has been very frus-

---

1. Quoted by Bernard Ramm, *The Christian View of Science and Scripture*, p. 173.

trating to these people. On the other hand, investigation has tended to corroborate the Biblical account. We will elaborate on this statement shortly; but first, let us consider the philosophical merit of the Genesis account.

(1) Agreement of the Bible Account With Good Philosophy

"In the beginning God created the heavens and the earth" (Genesis 1:1). The only alternative to a philosophy of ultimate creation is a philosophy of materialism. It is safe to say that a philosophy of materialism has never been held to be superior to that of idealism among the world's leading philosophers in general. Marx, Engels, and Nietzsche have had their day; but the philosophic consensus is that their philosophy does not measure up to the best standards.[2] Dr. Einstein, who may yet be counted by historians as of the stature of a philosopher, has said:

My religion consists of a humble admiration of the illimitable superior spirit who reveals himself in the slight details we are able to perceive with our frail and feeble minds. That deeply emotional conviction of the presence of a superior reasoning power, which is revealed in the incomprehensible universe, forms my idea of God.[3]

The fundamental idea of a creation is at least as agreeable to philosophy as the only other idea possible, that of the eternity of matter. It will be noticed here that in this respect theistic evolution is acceptable, for it teaches that originally there was Spirit, and the Spirit created matter. As concerns

---

2. Professor Durant, in describing the lives and opinions of seventeen of the greater philosophers from Plato to John Dewey, includes only six materialists. "It is astounding that so subtle a thinker and so ethereal a poet as Santayana should tie to his neck the millstone of a philosophy which after centuries of effort is as helpless as ever to explain the growth of a flower or the laughter of a child"—Will Durant, *The Story of Philosophy*, p. 371.

3. Quoted in *The Christian Science Monitor*, April 19, 1955.

most philosophy, theistic evolution is acceptable; but as concerns the facts of nature and the claims of the Scriptures, it is open to objections of the most serious kind.

(2) Agreement of the Bible Account With Facts of Science

Many geologists believe, from the abundance of igneous rock, that there was a time before life appeared on the planet when the earth was bathed in steam. If that is true, then there was a time when the waters of the earth were continuous from the bottom of the sea to the highest vapor. At first, very little if any light would penetrate this blanket of steam; but, as the earth cooled, the steam would become less dense until the time that diffused light could come through. The Bible considers this the end of the first stage. If originally the earth was bathed in steam, there did come a time when a clear stratum of air separated "the waters above" from "the waters beneath." The accomplishment of this constitutes the second age of the Bible account. The concept of "ages" is a somewhat arbitrary thing. Who can say precisely when one general condition ceases and a new one prevails? Actually the geologic ages merge into each other with little or no clear lines of demarcation, except the abrupt appearance of most of the great animal phyla in the Cambrian Period. Why should we be impatient with an ancient Hebrew prophet if he did not delineate the ages as we do today?

Geologists are not clear in their published works about the antecedence of plants or animals. There is evidence suggestive of pre-Cambrian plants; whereas they can only say that "probably" animals also existed.[4] Fenton suggests that plants may have been prerequisite to animal life because of the necessity of supplying free oxygen in the primeval atmos-

---

4. Carroll Lane Fenton, *Our Amazing Earth*, p. 273.

phere.[5] Ramm has pointed out that since the Bible does not intend to be encyclopedic in its outline, insects may have accompanied the creation of plants without this upsetting the general plan presented in Genesis.[6]

Plants would be happier in the thick, steamy air than animals. Though the light is now apparent on the earth, it is only as it comes through the envelope of steam which has risen to the upper atmosphere. The Bible indicates that next the sun, moon, and other luminaries appeared, which can mean that the steam finally condensed, allowing the light sources to be distinguishable.

According to Genesis the first animals were produced in the sea. Biology generally testifies to the accuracy of this position. The actuality of various types of primeval sea monsters is also attested by many fossils, such as that of the terrible Pleisaurus.

Palaeontology is in agreement with the Biblical account in introducing birds along with various kinds of sea monsters. Fenton indicates that in the Jurassic period: "Water reptiles and huge dinosaurs became common. First birds appeared. Mollusks were abundant."[7] He also indicates that dinosaurs were common in the period just preceding. But if you allow the Bible a slightly (as geological time goes) different grouping, it is legitimate to view the birds and water monsters as appearing in the same age. Remember that the Bible only professes to be giving a broad summary of the origins of living things.

The Bible account works up progressively to the most complex type of life in man. The creeping things of the earth would generally be more complex in organization than the animals of the sea. This accords with the facts of biology and geology.

---

5. *Ibid.*, p. 280.
6. Ramm, *op. cit.*, p. 218.
7. Fenton, *op. cit.*, p. 272.

The Bible strongly suggests that each kind of animal and plant is distinct from each other one and only reproduces after its kind. Mountains of labor have been expended to disprove this; but most biologists are agreeing reluctantly with Professor Richard Goldschmidt, of the University of California, who says: "Nowhere have the limits of the species been transgressed, and these limits are separated from the limits of the next good species by the unbridged gap, which also includes sterility."[8] Compare also the statement of Dr. Nils Heribert-Nilsson, of the Botanical Institute of Lund, Sweden:

Variants are formed, out crossed and arise anew in a kaleidoscopic sequence within the species. But the species remains the same sphere of variation. The various species will remain like circles that do not intersect. Species are constant.[9]

We have seen how that in several points the Bible account of the origin of things is in keeping with some of the best thinking of scientific men:

1. It is good philosophically.
2. The ideas of primeval darkness on the face of the earth caused by an envelope of steam, of a later lifting of this envelope, and still later, of its dispersion are acceptable to one geologic theory of the formation of the earth.
3. The statement of priority of plants to animals is in agreement with the actual evidence we have of early life.
4. The Bible accords with the facts of geology and biology in deriving the first animals from the sea.
5. The Bible correctly introduces living things in the order of their complexity.
6. Many years of biological research have corroborated the Bible claim for fixity of species.

---

8. Quoted in *Evolution, A Handbook for Students,* Anonymous, p. 62.
9. *Ibid.,* p. 27.

(3) Disagreement of the Evolutionary Account With Facts of Science

It has often been suggested that specialists in religion should stay with religious questions and shun involvement in questions of science. This is a good general principle. Some scientific generalizations, however, have implications which vitally affect religious teaching. When some men of science make philosophical interpretations of their data, it is the duty, as well as the right, of theologians to check the processes by which they arrived at those philosophical conclusions, especially if those conclusions are at variance with the philosophy which is being taught in the name of God by the theologians.

In fact, every human being is a student of the business of living a life. When propounding a philosophy of life, a scientist is no more a specialist than any other normal human being. When some scientists or their admirers tell a Christian that his fundamental explanation of life is wrong, it is altogether fitting for him to ask, "Why?" It is on this basis that the author, a layman to most science, makes bold to check on the evolutionary explanation which is urged on him and the people of his faith. Wherever there is well-established data, the author has determined humbly to accept it; but he reserves the right to debate with even a scientist on philosophical questions.

The objection that theologians are not trained in biology loses much of its force when we observe that much of the data of living things is outside the laboratory and open to all to inspect. The author has spent hours poring over shell collections and butterfly presses; he has counted the whiskers on the family cat and the geometric figures on the shell of the family turtle, and never misses an opportunity to visit a zoo. Anyone can look closely at the family pet, the summer-time butterflies, an egg in the kitchen, the pansies in the yard. Besides, encyclopedias are available to all. One does not have to be a biologist in order to be acquainted with a large cross section of the data of life.

It will be noticed that care has been taken in this study to avoid the impression of antagonism with scientists as such. It is not their techniques that are under criticism (the writer has long enjoyed the fruits of their labors), but the philosophy of *some* of them. In fact, many of the giants of scientific progress have been men who rejected the evolutionary explanation of life in favor of creation, among them: Adam Sedgwick, Darwin's teacher; Louis Pasteur, whose blessing in medicine we still enjoy; Louis Agassiz, who held to what he called Epochs of Creation; Michael Farraday, the father of modern physics; Charles M. A. Stine, for many years a director of research for du Pont; James D. Dana, of Yale University, a pioneer in North American geology; Sir William Dawson, Professor of Geology at McGill University; Professor Joseph LeConte, geologist of the University of California; Professor R. Virchow, the highest German authority on physiology; Lord Kelvin, British physicist; Sir Ambrose Fleming, for some years president of the Victoria Institute and Philosophical Society of Great Britain; and Sir Winston Churchill, a specialist in political science and history, besides others mentioned elsewhere in this chapter.

The scientific testimony given on the side of creation is not so voluminous as that for evolution; but it is as weighty. Nevertheless, the evolutionary explanation of the origin of things is often presented as well established by the findings of scientific investigation.[10] Indeed, many of the facts uncovered may be arranged in such a way as to convince an uncritical mind, especially if the interpretation is backed by

---

10. *Cf.* William H. Roberts, *The Problem of Choice*, p. 104: "The idea of evolution is both very ancient and very modern. It is at once one of the presuppositions of science and one of its supreme achievements." *Cf.* also Harry E. Fosdick, *The Modern Use of the Bible*, p. 215: ". . . today one must think in terms of evolution."

a preponderance of assent by reputable men of science. Most seasoned men of science know, however, though they may not say it, that the interpretation meets with serious objections before the mass of data which has been collected. Let us consider some of these objections.

a) LACK OF EXPERIMENTAL CONFIRMATION.—When we use this negative argument we are placing the fullest reliance upon the investigational techniques of scientists. It is not their scientific investigations that we object to—let these be encouraged in the fullest possible way—it is the evolutionary philosophy of some of them which we are calling to task. The theory of evolution lacks the feature most essential to its being placed upon a scientific basis. "Within the period of human history we do not know of a single instance of the transformation of one species into another one," declared T. H. Morgan, a Nobel Prize winner.[11] Experimental biology, despite mountainous labors, has failed to produce a step toward a higher species. By his own admission, all the fruit fly mutations produced by H. J. Muller were degenerate. Even if history be but a microscopic segment of evolutionary time, yet it is large enough before our eyes, living as we are in the midst of it, to afford some knowledge of the whole. A bacteriologist can tell the general extent of a disease in the eight or more quarts of blood in a person by examining a microscopic quantity of it. The dimensions of a circle can be determined from a very small arc from it. "A journey of a thousand miles begins with one step." A tiny man on an insignificant planet can measure the distance to a star many light years away. If there is a continuous trend in biological development, we should be able to detect it with only a small sampling of the whole. The author does not think the logic valid that when viewed in terms of millions of years our data must appear different from what it does when viewed in terms of thousands or hundreds. Dr. Heri-

---

11. Quoted by T. C. Innes, *Darwinism: Faith or Science?* p. 20.

bert-Nilsson says that "we are forced to this conclusion that the theory of evolution has not been verified by experimental investigations of the origin of species." [12] Professor Goldschmidt indicates that evolutionists cannot draw comfort from the suggestion that subspecies may be a beginning toward a new species:

The species limit is characterized by a gap, an unbridged difference in many characters. This gap cannot be bridged by theoretically continuing the subspecific gradient or cline beyond its actually existing limits. The subspecies do not merge into the species either actually or ideally . . . Subspecies are actually, therefore neither incipient species nor models for the origin of species. They are more or less diversified blind alleys within the species. [13]

b) THE RECORD OF THE ROCKS.—Nor does pre-history give better support to the theory. Douglas Dewar, a scientist of the Evolution Protest Movement, holds that there are no pre-Cambrian fossils extant, and that the fossil record opens suddenly in the lower Cambrian period with the presence of all the major animal phyla except the vertebrates.

Here then we have, on the one hand, the complete absence of indubitable fossils in all the rocks laid down before the Cambrian period, and on the other hand millions of fossils in the rocks of the Cambrian period and every later period. The natural explanation of this phenomenon is that there was a great creation of marine animals and plants at the beginning of the Cambrian period. Owing to the influence of Darwin modern biologists and palaeontologists mostly refuse to accept this explanation, and in consequence biology and geology have not kept pace with the exact sciences. Although the rocks of the Cambrian and all later periods abound in fossils, there are in every period some beds in which fossils are scarce or even entirely lacking, but such beds

---

12. *Hereditas*, p. 236, quoted in *Evolution, A Handbook for Students*, p. 60.
13. Richard Goldschmidt, *The Material Basis of Evolution*, p. 6, quoted in *Ibid.*, p. 62.

are rarely more than a few hundred feet thick, whereas the un-fossiliferous pre-Cambrian beds are thousands of feet thick.[14]

Moreover, as Dr. Dewar has argued, the transitional forms, being weaklings, should afford us the greater fossil remains, whereas they are practically absent. Sir J. William Dawson, Professor of Geology and Principal of McGill University, has stated the argument from geology very succinctly:

The record of the rocks is decidedly against evolutionists, especially in the abrupt appearance of new forms. Every grade of life was in its highest and best estate in the age when first introduced. Palaeontology furnishes no evidence as to the actual transformation of one species into another.[15]

One of the most objectionable habits of evolutionary teaching is that of presenting highly imaginative reconstructions in such a way that the uncritical would take them as realities. In Webster's Collegiate Dictionary, Piltdown man is defined in such a way as to give no indication that the idea was theoretical (now known to be based on fraud). Neanderthal man is always presented with his head thrust forward in the fashion of an ape, whereas it has lately been proved that he walked erect. Eohippus has everywhere been advanced as a transitional stage toward the horse. The Baroness Wentworth, a breeder of thoroughbred and Arab horses, writes of the exhibits of the horse in the American Museum of Natural History:

---

14. Douglas Dewar, *Transactions of the Victoria Institute*, 1948, p. 22, quoted in *ibid.*, p. 15. *Cf. Encyclopaedia Britannica*, Vol. 17, p. 106: "Pre-Cambrian deposits of the age of the Algonkian and Torridonian often exhibit traces of animal life in the form of tracks and burrows similar to those made by living marine 'worms,' but determinable remains of animals are exceedingly rare in them. C. C. Walcott has, however, described a small fauna from North America, which is remarkable for its resemblance to that which is found in the succeeding Lower Cambrian . . . In the Cambrian characteristic representatives of nearly all the phyla of the animal kingdom are found."

15. Quoted in a pamphlet by W. Bell Dawson, *Opinions of Scientists on Evolution*, p. 3.

This pictorial Evolutionary series . . . has been subjected to such wholesale fancy reconstruction of missing parts that, as presented to the public, its evidential value amounts to little more than that of a pictorial historical novel. . . . If we accept the reconstructions of Eohippus, his ribs were eighteen, Orohippus dropped to fifteen, Pliohippus jumped to nineteen, and Equus Scotti is back to eighteen. Eohippus starts at six or seven lumbars, Orohippus shows eight and, some five million years later, Equus Scotti is back at six! [16]

Doctor Austin Clark of the United States National Museum says that "no matter how far back we go in the fossil record of previous animal life upon the earth we find no trace of any animal forms which are intermediate between the various major groups or phyla." [17] When one considers the vast number of individuals presupposed by evolution to be in the many intermediate species, it is fair to suppose that some would have been found if they had been existent, what with more than a hundred years of diligent search by the evolutionists themselves.

c) THE SO-CALLED VESTIGIAL ORGANS.—Many physicians are extremely doubtful that any part of the human body is useless, or vestigial. In a Champaign, Illinois, newspaper article Dr. William Brady argues that tonsils are one of our best defenses against disease. It used to be held that there were over a hundred structures in man which are the remains of organs once required by our ancestral forms but now no longer essential. The number has diminished as our knowledge has increased. Now only a very few are listed, such as the appendix, the coccyx, the pineal gland, and the muscles of the outer ear. There is good reason to believe that these muscles are necessary to the efficient metabolism in the flesh of the outer ear. He would be rash indeed who would dogmatically deny a use to any of the other organs men-

---

16. *Thoroughbred Racing Stock*, p. 79, quoted in *Evolution, A Handbook for Students*, p. 55.
17. Austin Clark, *The New Evolution: Zoogenesis*, p. 189, quoted in *ibid.*, p. 17.

tioned above. It has been determined that the coccyx is necessary as a support for the muscles which control elimination.

d) ABSENCE OF NASCENT ORGANS.—There are no nascent organs in man, contrary to what one would expect if evolution were still in effect. In fact, there are no nascent organs anywhere in nature. Has evolution suddenly stopped? Dr. Julian Huxley suggests that it has: ". . . it seems probable that life's major trends have run their course." [18] But this is fatal to the very foundation of evolution, which is continuity. How could there be continuity for hundreds of millions of years and a sudden cessation of the process in our own age?

e) TECHNIQUES THAT COULD NOT HAVE BEEN GRADUAL DEVELOPMENTS.—The web-spinning of a spider would manifestly be impossible until the spinning mechanism was fully developed. Is it reasonable to suppose that the parts necessary to web-spinning would be added one by one until at last they began working together to perform this function?

A certain type of wasp, in order to provide food for its young, stings a caterpillar in just the right place, with just the right chemical, to paralyze without killing. The little wasps then feed on the live meat until they are able to provide for themselves. They never see the technique performed; yet when the proper time comes, the recently matured wasps re-enact the performance according to the needs of their own young. This technique had to be performed rightly in the first and every succeeding generation of wasps, or else there would be no wasps, for the young cannot survive without this preserved meat—dead meat would be fatal to them.

The beautiful golden plover has its mating grounds in the far Alaskan North. When the season is over, the birds take off en masse and make the five-thousand-mile trip over the trackless ocean to the Hawaiian Islands. What, or who,

---

18. *Endeavor,* January 1946, p. 12, quoted in *ibid.,* p. 37.

guides them? One may say that the group has learned through trial and error. But some of the birds are too young to make the trip with the main flight. They must wait until their wings are strong enough. Then these birds, which have never made the trip or seen it made, spring into the air and are guided unerringly over thousands of miles of open sea, without chart or compass, to some tiny dots of land in mid-Pacific, a navigational feat that is not equalled by man. This is evidence of a purpose which cannot be explained by evolution.

f) THE ELEMENT OF PURPOSE IN NATURE.—There are many evidences of conscious intention in the world about us. The tendons in the legs of tree-roosting birds are so entwined about their leg bones that when the birds squat to roost the weight of their bodies causes the feet to clasp the limb tightly so that the birds do not fall off when sleep relaxes their muscles. One would be hard put to show how blind chance could create such an effect. There is a great gap between a bird leg that can do this and one that cannot, a gap that cannot be bridged by a theory of gradual adaptation. The bird either stays on the limb, or he falls off—there are no gradations in-between.

A hen egg is a marvel of ingenuity. The yolk is constructed with the equilibrium of a battleship. No matter how much the egg is rolled, the yolk remains upright. It is anchored to one end of the egg by a rope of albumen, which acts as a swivel joint. In the other end of the egg is an air pocket, which provides the chick with just enough air to last until it can work its way out of the shell; that head end of the shell is softer than the rest. But the chick's bill is too soft to break even this part of the shell. So he is provided with a little hard cone over his beak with which he pecks his way out. Soon thereafter the cone falls off. Now, all these provisions were necessary the first time a chick was formed in a shell, or else there would be no chickens.

One of the strongest arguments for conscious provision in

nature is the fact that man is endowed with a brain of which he is able in a lifetime to use only a small part. Such an organ could not have been developed through use.

Another circumstance which weighs heavily against the chance idea of the development of the life of the world[19] is the presence of such a variety of things which serve the taste of man, without figuring in any real sense in his survival. Great masses of men in China, India, and elsewhere have survived and multiplied on a very simple diet. Yet in the world at large there are scores of things that please the taste of man, such as spices innumerable, pepper, nutmeg, cinnamon, ginger, allspice, turmeric, tartar, garlic; a world of distinctive-tasting and distinctively colored vegetables, lettuce, cabbage, beets, carrots, peas, squash, watermelon, eggplant, celery, kale, rutabagas, turnips, radishes, tomatoes; fruits galore, apples, oranges, pears, bananas, guavas, grapes, avocadoes, lemons, grapefruits; and many distinctively flavored meats, beef, pork, lamb, rabbit, frog, chicken, crab, oysters, shrimp, lobsters. It is incredible that such a wide variety of pleasant-looking, -tasting, and -smelling things just happened to be present to delight the palate of man and at the same time provide nourishment of many kinds (energy, body-building, vitamins, etc.) for him. One ought rather to lift up thankful eyes to the Designer who provided these things for the human soul's craving for variety.

Still another telling argument for a personal Designer of the animal world and against the theory of evolution is the omnipresence of symmetry.

> Tiger! Tiger, burning bright
> In the forests of the night,
> What immortal hand or eye
> Could frame thy fearful symmetry?
>
> —WILLIAM BLAKE

---

19. *Cf.* Albert Einstein in *The Christian Science Monitor*, April 19, 1955: "I cannot believe that God plays dice with the world."

Most of the members of the animal kingdom exhibit an oppositional symmetry that cannot be explained by chance. The author counted nine distinct colors on a small bird in a Chicago zoo; and each marking on one side was duplicated in reverse on the other. Do birds check for symmetry details when choosing a mate? A friend of the author has a collection of butterflies. It was noted that invariably the markings on one wing were duplicated in reverse on the other, even to the number of the many small circles on some. Every little zigzag, crevice, or protrusion on one wing was duplicated on the other. Do butterflies make a minute check on the markings of their wings before choosing mates? The author has noticed the same phenomenon in various ways and degrees on fishes, cats, birds, bugs, spiders, horses, dogs, cattle, hogs, sheep, lions, tigers, bears, wolves, caracals, etc. On the beautiful spotted turtle (*Clemmys cuttata*) there are thirteen bright dots in perfect symmetrical balance. There are smaller dots interspersed without being symmetrically balanced as far as minute examination is concerned, though the general effect is one of balance. This circumstance shows that the symmetry is not due to any folding of the embryo, a solution in keeping with evolution that has been advanced in explanation of the symmetry of the wings of the butterfly.

The author's wife is a shell collector. The ubiquitous things had begun to get in his hair until one day he began to see in them a wonder that is not apparent elsewhere in the wonderful, wonderful world. Some of the conical shells have regular gradations running in three different planes. This circumstance is inspiring enough; but it is staggering to recognize how these are formed. They are formed simultaneously, bit by bit, as the little fleshy creature grows around its axis in an ever-enlarging spiral.

A thoughtful physician has stated the case for purpose in a tremendous statement:

If, starting out with the ninety-two chemical elements and the cosmic forms of energy—heat, light, electricity, magnetism—it were possible for a planner deliberately to create an environment for the complex being we call the life-personality, an environment in which and out of which it gains its substance and energy, its security and perpetuation, it would be impossible to construct one better suited than that actually existing.[20]

Dr. Julian Huxley, formerly Director of the United Nations Educational, Scientific and Cultural Organization (UNESCO) seeks to account for the obvious purpose which we see in nature:

In conclusion we have the glorious paradox that this purposeless mechanism, after a thousand million years of its blind and automatic operations, has finally created purpose—as one of the attributes of our own species.[21]

The author can only ask, with a certain medical scientist, "Would it be unscientific to say that Julian Huxley's glorious paradox is more incredible than the concept of special creation?" [22] Even if his "glorious paradox" be believed, it does not account for the many evidences of purpose antecedent to man.

   g) THE DISINTEGRATING CHARACTER OF THE UNIVERSE.— Uranium is constantly breaking down into radium, which in turn is breaking down into a form of lead. The same process is generally true throughout the physical universe. Sir James Jeans compared the universe to a clock which is running down. Professor Frank Allen, of the University of Manitoba, has said:

The principles of physics without exception prove that the universe is in a process of running down, like a clock, and not of building up. No evidence of any kind in physics, chemistry or astronomy supports the theory of evolution.[23]

---

20. Louis Berman, *Behind the Universe*, p. 174.
21. *Rationalist Annual*, 1946, p. 87, quoted in *Evolution, A Handbook for Students*, p. 47.
22. *Ibid.*
23. Frank Allen, statement authorized for publication by himself, *ibid.*, p. 65.

Dr. Robert E. D. Clark, of Cambridge University, sees evolution as a contradiction of the law of entropy.

In face of these and many other examples, it would be reckless indeed to see in evolution a self-ordering principle of nature which runs contrary to the entropy law. If in other sciences observable events which seem to contradict this law are never taken at their face value, it is difficult indeed to see why a biological theory about non-observable events of past history should be given an altogether different status.[24]

Physicists testify to the generally disintegrating character of the universe; yet evolution assumes the self-organizing of matter.

h) ABSOLUTE FAILURE TO EXPLAIN LIFE.—Dr. Benjamin Minge Duggar, the discoverer of aureomycin, spent five years at the University of Wisconsin trying to make living matter out of nonliving. He put together all the necessary ingredients of living matter and subjected them to dozens of procedures calculated to produce life. Many others have worked with this fundamental problem with the same negative results. Anthropologist George Lechler concludes, "For me, I prefer the belief in a creator, divine, supernatural. I cannot accept chaos."[25] The scientist, in order to explain the origin of the obviously most important thing in nature, must call in the Creator-God of the Bible. But the strongest protagonist for evolution has said, "Evolution, if consistently accepted, makes it impossible to believe the Bible."[26] Thus, it turns out that in the most important element of nature, the Bible explanation of origins is superior to that of evolution.

i) ADVERSE PRACTICAL EFFECTS IN HUMAN HISTORY.—The evolutionary theory of origins is unsatisfactory because it has practical results bad for the human race. (Of course,

---

24. *Transactions of the Victoria Institute,* 1946, p. 62, quoted in *ibid.*, p. 66.

25. Quoted in an article in *Collier's* for August 11, 1951, by Howard Whitman, "What Scientists Believe," p. 60.

26. T. H. Huxley, quoted in a pamphlet, "This is Serious!" by Newman Watts, p. 1.

this thought involves the presumption that true philosophy is necessarily beneficent—few, if any, human minds would be satisfied to have it otherwise.) A major point of superiority of the Biblical explanation of the origin of things is in that a certitude-basis is given for ethical conduct, whereas evolution provides a very shaky and shifty basis indeed. When the fundamental reasons for good conduct are uncertain, men are prone to let expediency be the deciding factor. The Bible agrees with all the many evidences of design in testifying that the universe is existing because of God's purpose. This is an unmoving basis for moral conduct. The doctrine of blind chance has manifestly borne fruit in bloody carnage. Even philosophically, men cannot long be satisfied with the idea that the world is a "tale told by an idiot, full of sound and fury, signifying nothing." The doctrine of a personal, purposive, creative God is much more promising of successful living than that of a nebulous, impersonal force. Says H. G. Wells:

Prevalent people at the close of the nineteenth century believed that they prevailed by virtue of the Struggle for Existence, in which the strong and cunning get the better of the weak and confiding. . . . Hence a new scorn for the ideas of democracy that had ruled the earlier nineteenth century and a revived admiration for the overbearing and the cruel. . . . So the Darwinian crisis continued that destruction of Christian prestige . . . at a time when man's need for pacifying and unifying ideas was greater than it had ever been.[27]

E. W. Barnes, an ardent evolutionary churchman of Birmingham, England, admitted in a speech:

The actual, if unavowed, attitude of probably a large majority of men and women throughout Europe is that Evolution has banished God. We are (say those who are willing to lay bare their thoughts) transformed animals, and we must build the state on that knowledge.[28]

---

27. *The Outline of History*, pp. 421–25.
28. Quoted by Innes, *op. cit.*, p. 17.

Such was the attitude of Nazism and Fascism that bathed our world in blood; and such is the attitude of Communism that threatens to do it on a grander scale. Professor Will Durant affirms that Nietzsche, the father of Nazism, was the child of Darwin.[29] It is said that Marx wished to dedicate his *Das Capital* to Darwin.[30]

j) THE COELACANTH.—Perhaps the single exhibit most embarrassing to the evolutionary philosophy is the coelacanth fish. Said Leonard Carmichael, scientist-philosopher and head of the Smithsonian Institution:

A man can become downright philosophical over the coelacanth. We think of change as the order of things, yet man really hasn't changed in recorded time. He has changed tools, but I doubt if we are much smarter than a soldier in Hammurabi's army.

Still the philosophy of change is with us. It seems to me a wonder that the reproductive cells of the coelacanth have remained true. It seems unbelievable. Mountain ranges have grown and disappeared. Oceans have vanished but year after year the coelacanth has remained an example of biological conservatism and stability.[31]

The several living specimens caught recently off Madagascar are identical to fossil remains 300,000,000 years old!

(4) Dissatisfaction of Many Scientists With the Evolutionary Explanation

The purpose of this chapter has been to show that the Bible explanation of origins excels over the evolutionary explanation, the only other one in current favor. It is a fact not generally known that the theory of evolution has been remarkably unsatisfying to many of its strongest protagonists. According to Sir Edward Poulton of Oxford, T. H.

---

29. *Op. cit.,* p. 301.

30. *Cf.* Geoffrey West, *Charles Darwin, the Fragmentary Man,* p. 316, quoted by T. C. Innes, *op. cit.,* p. 18.

31. Article, "Scientist's 7 Modern Wonders of World," *St. Louis Post Dispatch,* July 11, 1954.

Huxley "was at no time a convinced believer in the theory he protected."[32] Charles Darwin says:

In my Journal I wrote that whilst standing in the midst of the grandeur of a Brazilian forest, "it is not possible to give an adequate idea of the higher feelings of wonder, admiration, and devotion which fill and elevate the mind." I well remember my conviction that there is more in man than the mere breath of his body. But now the grandest scenes would not cause any such convictions and feelings to rise in my mind. It may be truly said that I am like a man who has become color-blind, and the universal belief by men of the existence of redness makes my present loss of perception of not the least value as evidence.[33]

W. E. Ritter, Professor of Zoology at the University of California, writes that one can:

. . . hardly fail to see signs that the whole battle-ground of evolution will have to be fought over again; this time not so much between scientists and theologians, as among scientists themselves.[34]

Said D. H. Scott, of London University:

. . . we can no longer enjoy the comfortable assurance which once satisfied so many of us, that the main problem has been solved—all is again in the melting pot. . . . We have indeed a wealth of accumulated facts, but from the point of view of the theory of descent, they raise more questions than they solve.[35]

Sir William Bateson, addressing the American Association for the Advancement of Science in 1921, said: "The more our knowledge is extended the more incompatible does the theory of evolution become with the facts."[36]

---

32. *Essays on Evolution*, p. 193, quoted in *Evolution, A Handbook for Students*, p. 45.
33. Quoted by Innes, *op. cit.*, p. 6.
34. *Ibid.*, p. 25.
35. *Ibid.*, p. 22.
36. Quoted in "Opinions of Scientists on Evolution," a pamphlet by W. Bell Dawson, p. 2.

Sir Arthur Keith, one of the most influential proponents of evolution, makes the melancholy statement:

It was expected that the embryo would recapitulate the features of its ancestors from the lowest to the highest forms in the animal kingdom. Now that the appearances of the embryo at all stages are known, the general feeling is one of disappointment; the human embryo at no stage is anthropoid in its appearance.[37]

No supporter of the idea of creation has had to make an admission so damaging as these. How can we hold as the basic philosophy of life an idea which is so unsatisfying to our quest for the correlation of the data of life?

Over against this theory which has so little basis in fact, which is unsatisfying to its own adherents, and which has such disastrous practical effects, there is another explanation which excels in every respect. "Where did all things come from?" man asks. "From the Will of God," answers the Bible. And this is agreeable to the known facts of the composition of the universe. One physicist defined electricity as "a thought in the mind of God." Gravity is an inexplicable force. From the interrelation of these two come all the things in the universe. "By faith we understand that the worlds have been framed by the word of God," say the Scriptures.[38] No explanation has been offered that is as compatible to all the known scientific facts. "In the beginning God created (made from nothing) the heavens and the earth." We now know that the universe "hath not been made out of things which appear," as the Bible said centuries ago.[39] Centuries before the day of modern science, the Bible gave the proper order of the geological ages. "Where did all the various species come from?" asks man. Evolution answers, "The more complex came from the simpler." The Bible answered

---

37. *The Human Body,* p. 94, quoted in *Evolution, A Handbook for Students,* p. 67.
38. Hebrews 11:3.
39. *Ibid.*

centuries ago, "God spoke them each into separate existence and ordained that each reproduce after its kind." After a century of diligent inquiry, men of science are saying, "The various species will remain like circles that do not intersect. Species are constant." [40] It can only be a mark of its supernatural origin that the Bible at the dawn of human history has given a satisfactory explanation of the source of things whereas man through centuries of skilled and persistent investigation of nature has been unable to do so.

---

40. Nils Heribert-Nilsson, *Hereditas*, p. 232, quoted in *Evolution, A Handbook for Students*, p. 27.

Chapter VI ❧ *The Bible speaks with accuracy concerning scientific facts known to man only in recent times.*

SCIENTIFIC ACCURACY

It is to be emphasized from the first in this connection that this accuracy is more negative than positive, that is to say, it is more a matter of avoiding scientific error than of disclosing scientific truths which man could discover only by long, painstaking effort. A wise apologist for the Bible has well stated the reason for this:

God's wisdom in revelation is manifested to us in that he does not give us the knowledge which man, created in the image of God, can acquire by patient and accurate observation of the things of nature. A revelation of that type of truth would prove to be a hindrance rather than a help. Suppose that all scientific truth had been given to us by special revelation instead of by accurate, patient and continuous research. Would this not have impeded instead of encouraged the cultivation of man's intellect? The injunction to subdue the earth, which God gave to Adam, is applicable to all fields of human endeavor.[1]

Professor Ramm is even more insistent:

Our summary is but a restatement of our premise that the Holy Spirit conveyed infallibly true theological doctrines in the cultural mold and terms of the days of the Bible writers, and did not give to the writers the secrets of modern science. It is a misunderstanding of the nature of inspiration to seek such secrets in various verses of the Bible. However, contrary to liberalism, we affirm that the theological does at times overlap the scientific, e.g., matter is not eternal but created; the simple preceded the complex in the order of life; man is the latest and highest creation

---

1. John De Vries, *Beyond the Atom*, p. 93.

of God; Jesus was actually born of a virgin; or, the universe will have a demise and make way for the new heavens and the earth. But to look for relativity theory or nuclear physics or atomic theory is something far different.[2]

It has been repeatedly stated, and justifiably so, that the Bible is not a scientific textbook, but is the guidebook for the spiritual and moral life. The genealogies which are included are discouraging enough (though not without spiritual value) without the Bible's being written in scientific language. In II Kings 2:23 it is indicated that Elisha was bald. Suppose that instead of saying so in popular language the Bible had said:

He possessed no follicle appendages on the cutaneous apex of his cranial structure, anterior to the sagittal suture and posterior to the lambdoidal suture, where said follicle appendages habitually germinate.[3]

The proper direction of the soul is the business of all men. The Bible is written in language that can be grasped by all.

There are times, however, when the purposes of the Bible writings necessitate allusion to natural facts. The striking thing is that whereas other religious writings plainly make gross errors when viewed in the light of modern knowledge, the Biblical statements on nature are always correct. Let us compare the cosmogony of various religions with that of the Bible.

The Babylonians taught that the God Marduk slew the primeval monster Tiamat and made the earth out of her carcass. The Egyptians thought that men were hatched out of the white worms left by the overflow of the Nile.

The idea of the original earth-stuff being an egg is found in several ancient religions. The Polynesians believed the Heaven-god laid an egg on the waters which became the earth.[4] The Indian Manu tells of a golden egg hatching

---

2. Bernard Ramm, *The Christian View of Science and Scripture*, p. 136.
3. Harry Rimmer, *The Harmony of Science and Scripture*, p. 62.
4. *The Encyclopaedia Britannica*, Eleventh Edition, Vol. 7, p. 216.

out a god, Brahmana, who is the progenitor of the worlds.[5] One ancient Egyptian religious cosmogony has it that the artisan-god Ptah broke the egg (of the world) with his hammer.[6]

It must be said that Zoroastrianism approaches the nobility of the Biblical account, for there is little of the grossness we find in the other accounts. According to the *Avesta*, good and bad spirits each created their respective spirit followers. The good spirit created the material world out of nothing.[7] Apparently, however, the Zoroastrian concept of the sky was unscientific, for Zoroaster prays: "This I ask thee, Ahura, Who upheld the earth beneath and the firmament from falling?"[8] In the Hebrew Scriptures the word for firmament is "expanse" and consequently there is no suggestion that it might fall.

In Greek mythology the earth and the heavens are supported on the shoulders of the god Atlas. The ancient Greek religion thought that the sun and the moon arose out of the ocean.[9] It also alludes to the egg-idea. "Love (Eros) issued from the egg of Night, which floated on Chaos."[10] Also it is taught that the earth floats on the primeval waters.[11]

The Hindus taught that "the second Avatar was in the form of a Tortoise, which form he assumed to support the earth when the gods were churning the sea for the beverage of immortality, Amrita."[12]

In the mythology of the Northmen, a cow, by licking the ice, formed first the hair, then the head, and then the whole body of a god, who then proceeded to slay the frost-giant Ymir and to make of his body the earth.[13]

---

5. *Ibid.*
6. *Ibid.*
7. *Ibid.*
8. Lewis Browne, *The World's Great Scriptures,* p. 366.
9. Thomas Bulfinch, *Bulfinch's Mythology,* p. 8.
10. *Ibid.,* p. 9.
11. *Ibid.,* p. 15.
12. *Ibid.,* p. 256.
13. *Ibid.,* pp. 262–63.

The Alaskan Indians had a story of a crow incubating a human mask into a man.[14] The Thlinkit Indians of the Northwest relate that the god Yehl (Raven) stole the sun, the moon, and the stars out of a box.[15] The Algonkins said Michabo (the Great Hare) made men of carcasses of dead animals.[16]

The Incas of Peru held that the creator and the "mother-egg" became the sun and the moon respectively.[17]

When we compare these unscientific ideas[18] with the cosmogony of the Bible we can understand why Wilbur Smith was led to say: "Genesis is the only book of antiquity which is ever considered when discussing the scientific accuracy of ancient literature on the creation of the world."[19]

a) METEOROLOGY.—The Bible usually avoids making statements about natural law. With the variety of subjects and circumstances which it discusses, however, it is inevitable that it should sometimes touch on matters of natural fact and law. The striking observation is that it always does so accurately, not so much in the positive statement of the laws of science, but in avoiding scientific error in the natural discussions which are incidental to, but also necessary to, some of its theological messages.

Job touches the field of meteorology when he writes of the "weight of the wind" (28:35). Are we to suppose that it was at that time a matter of common knowledge that the air has weight? The ancients did not know that rain is formed from the moisture which evaporates from the surface of the earth; yet the Psalmist states this principle correctly (Psalm 135:6–7).

---

14. *Encyclopaedia Britannica,* Eleventh Edition, Vol. 7, p. 215.
15. *Ibid.*
16. *Ibid.*
17. *Ibid.*
18. Possibly excepting the *Avesta.* The Bible gives some credibility to Zoroastrianism, for it indicates that the Magi, Zoroaster's followers, supernaturally learned the time and country of Messiah's birth (Matthew 2:1 ff.).
19. *Therefore, Stand,* p. 329.

Solomon exhibits a superhuman knowledge of meteorology when he says:

The wind goeth toward the south, and turneth about unto the north; it turneth about continually in its course, and the wind returneth again to its circuits. All the rivers run into the sea, yet the sea is not full; unto the place whither the rivers go, thither they go again. (Ecclesiastes 1:6–7)

If this were a mythological work, we would expect the writer to say that some god puffed up and blew the wind whenever it was felt. How did the Scripture writer know that the air that moves as wind may return again as wind from another direction, and that there are regular patterns which the great air currents of the world follow? Comparing his statement in verse seven with the Psalmist's phraseology above, we may conclude that he was led to allude accurately to the cycle of evaporation and condensation which fills our rivers but does not overflow the ocean.

b) ASTRONOMY.—As for astronomy, Professor Ramm implies that the book of Job supernaturally speaks of the chains of Pleiades, for the streams of nebulous matter connecting the stars of this constellation are only seen by modern telescopic equipment.[20] Job correctly explains the support of the earth when he says: "He hangeth the earth upon nothing" (26:7). Here we have nothing of cosmic seas, or turtles, or pillars, or Atlases. That the earth hangs upon nothing is as good a statement as can be made in popular language of the suspension of the earth.

Isaiah represents God as sitting "above the circle of the earth" (40:22), which is most smoothly interpreted as an allusion to the shape of the earth, although some would explain it as meaning that the area within one's view at any given locality forms a rough circle. The book of Isaiah, however, everywhere speaks of God in the most magnificent terms and would hardly refer to him as observing only a

---

20. Ramm, *op. cit.*, p. 143.

limited portion of the earth. The very context requires the view that he have within his ken the whole earth.

Solomon, at the dedication of his temple, said that "heaven and the heaven of heavens cannot contain thee; how much less this house that I have builded!" (II Chronicles 6:18.) Here we have allusion to the concept that there are many starry universes, and that they are related in one vast system, which thought is one of the most thrilling challenges of modern astronomy and physics to prove.

c) OCEANOGRAPHY.—There are places in mid-ocean where it is possible to obtain fresh water. There are "springs of the sea," of which God told Job (38:16) centuries before men perfected the equipment to find them. Millennia before man was able to discover the variegated contour of the ocean floor, Job wrote of the "recesses of the deep" (38:16).

d) BIOLOGY.—The Bible has described in popular language scores of plants and animals; and these descriptions have proved accurate. The description and prescribed treatment of disease in Leviticus 13 reads like a page from a medical journal, except for the popular language.

e) GEOLOGY.—In the matter of geology, the Bible correctly states that mountains were once covered by water (Psalm 104:6), that water had a prominent role in the formation of the surface of the land (II Peter 3:5), that deserts were once inhabited (Psalm 107:33–34), that mountains have been overturned and rivers have been cut through solid rock (Job 28:9–10).

Against the evolutionary view in vogue a generation ago that all cells were essentially the same, the Bible tells us (accurately, we now know) that "all flesh is not the same flesh: but there is one flesh of men, and another flesh of beasts, and another flesh of birds, and another of fishes" (I Corinthians 15:39). There is a reagent once known as "Antihuman Preciptin," with which it is easy to tell whether a piece of flesh is animal or human.[21]

---

21. Harry Rimmer, *The Harmony of Science and Scripture*, p. 109.

Much has been said for and against the impact of the argument from scientific accuracy; but when the debatings have exhausted themselves and all the extreme statements have been eliminated, there is still substantial evidence for the supernatural origin of the Hebrew-Christian Scriptures in the broad fact that they consistently avoid scientific error in their many discussions of natural phenomena.

CHAPTER VII ❧ *The Bible contains a number of predictions which have been fulfilled in ways that preclude human foreknowledge.*

PREDICTION AND ITS FULFILLMENT

DESPITE THE FACT that it is popular in some circles to discount almost entirely the predictive element in the Bible, the Bible authors gave it considerable importance. Consider the instruction of Moses:

And if thou say in thy heart, How shall we know the word which Jehovah hath not spoken? When a prophet speaketh in the name of Jehovah, if the thing follow not, nor come to pass, that is the thing which Jehovah hath not spoken: the prophet hath spoken it presumptuously, thou shalt not be afraid of him (Deuteronomy 18:21–22)

According to this Mosaic utterance the one distinguishing mark of a genuine prophet is his ability to predict correctly. In the latter portion of Isaiah's prophecy that greatest of all Old Testament prophets declares that Jehovah's ability (1) to explain the origin of the universe ("former things," *i.e.,* in the Hebrew literally "head things," or "origin things") and (2) to predict the distant future prove that he is the God and that the other gods are nonentities, for they can do neither. Compare also:

Produce your cause, saith Jehovah; bring forth your strong reasons, saith the King of Jacob. Let them bring them forth, and declare unto us what shall happen: declare ye the former things, what they are, that we may consider them, and know the latter end of them; or show us things to come. Declare the things that are come hereafter, that we may know that ye are gods. . . . (Isaiah 41:21–23)

Some people today feel that since there is considerable antipathy to the predictive evidence for the inspiration of the scriptures, we ought to refrain from using it. Although it is true that it is immediately offensive to some habits of mind, it does not seem in the interests of truth in the long run to disregard the fact that the Bible itself uses it. Indeed, Isaiah speaks of prediction and its fulfillment as a "strong reason" for accepting Jehovah as the true God. Let us observe some particular cases that go to make up this strong reason for the validity of the writings of Jehovah's prophets.

a) Fulfilled Prediction in the Area of National Affairs.—A marvelous instance is that of the Dispersion or Scattering of Israel: ". . . if thou wilt not hearken unto the voice of Jehovah thy God . . . Jehovah will cause thee to be smitten before thine enemies . . . and thou shalt be tossed to and fro among all the kingdoms of the earth" (Deuteronomy 28:15, 25). Moses wrote these words in the fifteenth century b.c. In 721 b.c., after repeated prophetical warning, the Northern Kingdom of Israel fell and the people were scattered; in 586, after repeated warnings, the Southern Kingdom fell and the people were scattered, to be returned under the Persians. Then, in a.d. 70, the most terrible scattering came about after Titus destroyed Jerusalem after breaking the Judaean rebellion against Rome. We today have witnessed this "tossing to and fro among all the kingdoms of the earth." "Everywhere the Jew," the world-traveler may say—it is a unique phenomenon among the nations of the world.

There are particulars in this prediction which have been exactly carried out. Moses warns that if Israel is disobedient, the day will come that "the tender and delicate woman" shall eat her own children because of the siege" (Deuteronomy 28: 56–57). This happened in the siege of Samaria in 594 b.c., when Jehoram was king (II Kings 6:26–29); and again in the siege of Jerusalem in a.d. 70, a noblewoman under stress of famine committed the same horrible act.[1]

Another particular is expressly stated: "And Jehovah

---

1. Flavius Josephus, *Wars of the Jews,* Book VI, Chapter III, par. 4.

will bring thee into Egypt again with ships . . ." (Deuteronomy 28:65). This happened when the Romans sold 97,000 of the Jews into Egyptian slavery after the destruction of Jerusalem in A.D. 70.[2]

In 721 B.C. Isaiah foretold to Hezekiah, king of Judah, that

. . . all that is in thy house, and that which fathers have laid up in store until this day, shall be carried to Babylon: nothing shall be left, saith Jehovah. And of thy sons that shall issue from thee, whom thou shalt beget, shall they take away; and they shall be eunuchs in the palace of the king of Babylon.

This is in chapter 39, which claims that Isaiah spoke these words. This prediction came at a time when Assyria, not Babylon, was the world power. How literally all this happened in the period around 586 B.C.! All the treasures of Judaea and most of the royalty and nobility were taken captive to Babylon.

A little later, yet before Babylonia was mistress of the world, Isaiah prophesied there would come a time when she would be queen of the world, but that she would be cast suddenly into the dust by a phenomenal new power. Cyrus the Great brought this to pass about 536, which was one hundred and seventy years later than the utterance of the prophecy.

Jeremiah, among many other wonderful prophecies, foretold the length of the captivity—seventy years—and that at the end of that time Babylon would fall (Jeremiah 25:11–12). The first captives left Judaea for Babylon in 606 B.C. At Cyrus' decree in 536 (seventy years later) the first exiles returned. Surely this is not mere human wisdom.

Ezekiel prophesied that Tyre would be desolated and become a bare rock—a place for the spreading of nets (chapter 26). Alexander the Great in 333 B.C. was so enraged at the obstinate and haughty resistance of Tyre that he ordered the whole city pushed into the sea. The very soil was swept

---

2. *Ibid.*, Chapter IX, par. 2.

into the water. Now the soil-less rocks are actually used as a place to spread out and dry fishing nets. Surely this fore-knowledge cannot be explained as human wisdom.

Daniel (chapter 8) foretells that Greece would succeed Medio-Persia as the world ruler, and that the first and illustrious king of this empire would be succeeded by four lesser men. It is well known that the brilliant Alexander left no successor and that his empire was divided among four of his generals. How did Daniel know this? A man writing during the Medio-Persian ascendancy could not have foreseen these things humanly. That is why those who dislike the predictive element in the Scriptures refer the book of Daniel to a later date. Their argument goes like this: "There is no supernatural prediction in the Bible. For Daniel to have foretold the Greek succession of rule would be supernatural. Therefore, Daniel did not write the book." But it is apparent that this is begging the question. They assume the thing that is in question—whether or not there is a supernatural element in the Bible. But, apart from any assumption, the facts support the authenticity of Daniel.

Returning to the prophet Isaiah, we find that he has told some things concerning Israel that from human reasoning a Hebrew could not tell about his people. The prophet was writing in the eighth century B.C.[3] when Judaea was still intact as a sovereign kingdom. Yet he implies that the Jews will be scattered all over the world, and he states:

I will bring thy seed from the east, and gather thee from the west; I will say to the north, Give up; and to the south, Keep not back; bring my sons from afar, and my daughters from the end of the earth; every one that is called by my name . . . (Isaiah 43:5–7)

If this was only a guess on his part, it was a remarkably accurate guess, for the Jews *were* scattered to every nation under the sun; and in our own generation, they have returned from every direction to their homeland of Palestine

---

3. *Cf.* Oswald T. Allis, *The Unity of Isaiah.*

and have re-established themselves as a state. No matter what feelings one may have about prediction in the Bible, these events are remarkable in the extreme.

b) Fulfilled Prediction in the Area of Personal Affairs.—There is another amazing prediction which came to pass three hundred and fifty years after its utterance. The record goes that a prophet spoke against Jeroboam, king of Israel, that a descendant of David, Josiah by name, would pollute the heathen altar by burning human bones upon it (I Kings 13:1 ff.). Jewish history records that a Davidic king namel Josiah destroyed that heathen shrine, and as perchance he spied the sepulchres of the heathen priests, he commanded that their bones should be burned upon the altar, thus rendering the place unfit for a heathen shrine thenceforth (II Kings 23:15–16). The chief argument the skeptics make against this as evidence is that it is impossible. But we ought to lay aside dogmatism and let the facts speak for themselves.

That marvelous prophet Isaiah was privileged to call the name of the king who should deliver Israel from the Babylonian captivity over 100 years before his birth (chapters 44–45). He foretells that Cyrus will make a phenomenal flash to world power, will easily enter the citadels of his enemies, will quickly seize upon fabulous riches thought untouchable, will return the Jewish captives, help rebuild Jerusalem and the temple, and all this, unbeknown to him, because Jehovah purposes it. All this, we know from secular history, Cyrus did. There is no book outside the Bible that can rival this prophecy as a proof of its divine origin.

c) Predictions of the Messiah.—Through the pages of the Jewish scriptures there runs a stream that goes like this: God will send his Anointed One into the earth to turn darkness into light, to proclaim liberty to the captives, to turn defeat into victory, to bring peace instead of trouble. His name shall be called Wonderful Counselor, the Mighty God, the Everlasting Father, the Prince of Peace.

In the days of Isaiah the prophet, Pekah, king of Israel,

and Rezin, king of Syria, conspired against Ahaz, king of Judah. Jehovah told Ahaz not to worry, for he would not allow the conspiracy to prosper, and offered to give the king a sign in confirmation. However, since Ahaz had already made up his mind to ask Tiglath-Pilezer of Assyria to help him, he refused to ask the sign. Then Jehovah said through Isaiah, ". . . the Lord himself shall give you a sign: Behold, a virgin shall conceive and bear a son, and shall call his name Immanuel" (7:14). The Hebrew word for virgin is rendered in the Greek Old Testament by the word *parthenos,* which means what we commonly mean when we say "virgin." It is 2,700 years since Isaiah's prophecy, and there has been no historical person recorded to be born of a virgin, except one—Jesus of Nazareth. Both Matthew and Luke testify that he was born without a human father.

In Micah 5:2 the very birthplace of the Coming One is announced.

But thou, Bethlehem Ephratah, though thou be little among the thousands of Judah, yet out of thee shall he come forth unto me that is to be ruler in Israel; whose goings forth have been from of old, from everlasting.

This was interpreted by the ancient Jews to refer to the coming of the Messiah, or the Christ, to use the Greek equivalent of the Hebrew word. So, in the New Testament account, when Herod asks the chief priests and scribes of the Jews where Messiah should be born, they answer, Bethlehem of Judaea, and quote the passage in Micah as proof.

Psalm 2, called Messianic by the most ancient Rabbinical writings, tells us that the Messiah or Christ will be the Son of God in a unique sense.

I will declare the decree: the Lord hath said unto me, Thou art my Son; this day have I begotten thee . . . Kiss the Son, lest he be angry, and ye perish from the way, when his wrath is kindled but a little. Blessed are all they that put their trust in him.

Jesus very definitely said, "I am the Son of God" (John 10:35).

Zechariah tells that Messiah is to be betrayed by his own familiar friend and even states the price for the betrayal.

And I said unto thee, If ye think good, give me my price: and if not, forbear. So they weighed for my price thirty pieces of silver, and cast them to the potter in the house of the Lord. (11:12–13)

It is a well-attested fact that one of the close friends of Jesus, Judas by name, betrayed him into the hands of his enemies, and that he did it for thirty pieces of silver, and that he did, in remorse, cast them down in the temple, and furthermore, that the money was used to buy the potter's field.

The Servant Poems of Isaiah have long been recognized in Jewish tradition as pertaining to Messiah. One of these (chapter 50) states that Messiah "gave my back to the smiters, and my cheeks to them that plucked off the hair: I hid not my face from shame and spitting." The four gospels record that Jesus suffered mistreatment in just such ways as these before the Sanhedrin and before the Roman soldiers.

Another Servant Poem (Isaiah 52:13–53:12) tells us that the face of Messiah is to be so marred as to make him an astonishment to all who should see him. Let us notice some of the things that happened to the face of Jesus through the night before his death. In the garden he prayed in such agony that the blood came out of the pores of the skin of his face. The mob came and took him away before there was time for him to clean the blood and dust off his face. It dried there. After the decision of the Jewish court, some of the crowd that was there spit in his face. That dried there too. Then the rabbis conceived a cunning game—they blindfolded him and kept striking him and asking him to prophesy who struck him. The blows from their hands and their fists certainly brought many ugly bruises to the face of Jesus. His visage was so marred . . . Then Pilate scourged him. Then the soldiers pressed a plaited crown of thorns upon his brow and bruised his head some more with a reed. The blood from the pricks of the thorns and the dirty spit from the mouths of the soldiers once more mingled on the face of the One who was called the Messiah.

The same Servant Poem asserts that Messiah is to be numbered with the transgressors at the time of his death, but that he would be buried with the rich. Again Jesus fulfills this Messianic requirement, for the gospels record that he was crucified between two criminals, but was buried in the tomb of a rich man, Joseph of Arimathea.

David, in the twenty-second Psalm, says a very mysterious thing: "for dogs have compassed me: the assembly of the wicked have inclosed me: they pierced my hands and my feet." There is no record of David's hands and feet ever being pierced. Evidently this Psalm is a prophecy of Messiah, the Promised One, as the early rabbis regarded it. And who then was the one to fill this part of the role of Messiah to have his hands and his feet pierced? Jesus is the only recognized Messiah who suffered in this manner. Jesus avoided death by stoning several times and once escaped from those who would have thrown him over a cliff; but when the proper time came, he willingly allowed them to nail him to a Roman cross.

Most important of all is the prophetic stipulation that the Messiah would suffer in lieu of the sufferings of others. With what repetition and clarity does the prophet Isaiah bring this out when he says:

Surely *he* has bourne *our* griefs, and carried *our* sorrows. *He* was wounded for *our* transgressions, bruised for *our* iniquities, The chastisement of *our* peace was upon *him;* and with *his* stripes *we* are healed. [The pronouns are emphatic in the Hebrew.]

All we like sheep have gone astray; we have turned every one to his own way, And the Lord hath laid on him the iniquity of us all. For the transgression of my people was he stricken.

It pleased the Lord to bruise him; he hath put him to grief; When thou shalt make his soul an offering for sin . . . for he shall bear their iniquities . . . he bare the sin of many, and made intercession for the transgressors. (Isaiah 53:4 ff.)

Jesus said, "The Son of Man came . . . to give his life a ransom for many" (Matthew 20:28). "I am the good shepherd: the good shepherd layeth down his life for the sheep." No one taketh it away from me, but I lay it down of myself. I have power to lay it down, and I have power to take it again" (John 10:11, 18.)

Lastly, the prophetic picture of the coming Messiah includes that his body will not undergo corruption in death as do the bodies of others. Says David, "For thou wilt not leave my soul in hell; neither wilt thou suffer thine Holy One to see corruption" (Psalm 16:10). Now David is dead; and his body has decayed. He was not speaking of himself, but of the Messiah. All the New Testament writers testify, as do many of the second-generation Christians, that Jesus of Nazareth arose bodily from the grave after his crucifixion.

Jesus was born four hundred years after the last Old Testament prophetical writing. If Jesus was born of a virgin in the town of Bethlehem, if he was introduced to Israel by an Elijah-like person as Malachi had said, if he claimed to be the Son of God and manifested powers to prove it, if he was mistreated and his face was bruised as the prophets had said that the Messiah's would be, if he was numbered with the transgressors, if he claimed that his awesome death was a ransom for many, if his resurrection is an established fact, this constitutes the strongest evidence that the men who foretold these things about him were divinely moved to do so.

This is too strong a structure to tear down by a mere flat denial of supernatural prediction. The authenticity of these writings is being attested more and more every day by objective scholarship. The fulfillment of these predictions is a matter of historical record. Let us then not timidly throw away one of the strongest of all arguments for the validity of our Biblical faith. The evidence of fulfilled prediction is here to stay.

Chapter VIII ❧ *The Hebrew-Christian Scriptures consistently place full blame upon humanity for failure to produce a righteous society on earth. We would not expect human nature to claim failure for itself. All other philosophies tend to excuse man.*

THE FAILURE OF SOCIETY

ALMOST ALL serious human reflection upon the subject has either explicitly or tacitly admitted that in the total picture mankind has fallen far short of a reasonable fulfillment of his own standards for what life on earth should be. According to an astute observation in a well-known American magazine:[1]

(1) More people in the world live in huts of mud and straw than any other shelter.

(2) More people travel on their own feet, or on the backs of small animals than in any other fashion.

(3) More people have a life expectancy of half our years (in the U.S.A.) than of any other figure.

(4) More mothers watch half their children die than see all their children reach maturity.

(5) More people live without the help of a doctor than those who have even rudimentary care.

(6) More eat what they themselves grow and starve if there is no harvest than obtain food in any other way.

(7) Most people do not know what it means really to vote.

These dismal conditions prevail after some six or eight thousand years of human civilization. Arnold Toynbee likens the twenty-one human civilizations to wretches climbing the side of a mountain, with far more failures than successes. He devotes much of his writing to such themes as "The Break-

---

1. Dickey Chapelle, "There'll Be No Christmas for Them," *Saturday Evening Post,* December, 1953.

downs of Civilizations" and "The Disintegrations of Civilizations." [2] To be sure, some have the roseate notion that it
matters not how many civilizations fail if we maintain the
hope that the ultimate effect of human progress will be
Utopia. It is to be doubted, however, that this thought is
much consolation to the millions of persons who will have
lived and died in abject misery in the long and dreary
process.

Besides, in the thoughts of many observing people there
is serious doubt that mankind is making progress as a whole
toward a happier way of life. We have more gadgets; but
we also have more gastronomic disturbances. Can anyone
contend that the ratio of happiness to misery is any greater
in the human race today than it was four thousand years
ago? More than a hundred thousand Japanese died in a
few seconds from bombs produced by twentieth-century ingenuity. Now we face the prospect that many millions will
die in a few hours if some spark touches off a third world
war. This we are told by the men most illuminated by the
accumulated knowledge of twenty centuries.[3] A recent
secular newspaper editorial anticipates a possible time of
tribulation such as mankind has never experienced. You
don't hear much talk of a Utopian society lately. Most world-
views which are being heard, including those based on the
Bible, give expression to the grotesque realities in which we
find ourselves; but there is one significant difference between
the Bible view of human society and that of all other
thought-systems. The Bible lays the blame squarely on the
corrupt nature of man; the others seek to excuse him.

---

2. *A Study of History.*
3. *Cf.* Albert Einstein's "last testament" warning that another war
would "threaten the existence of mankind," *Christian Science Monitor,* July
11, 1955. Eight other world-famous natural scientists signed the document.

(1) Non-Christian Answers

Islam denies that man's nature is evil. Its extreme fatalism tends to make God's will the author of the evil conditions of society; and Mohammedans are in the habit of excusing themselves for them. The Koran makes Allah to say:

If we had pleased, we had certainly given unto every soul its direction; but the word which hath proceeded from me must necessarily be fulfilled when I said, Verily, I will fill hell with genii and with men altogether.[4]

While the *Hindu* scriptures do have much to say about sin, yet the basic Hindu ideas of *karma* (by which it is meant that all the individual's acts are only temporary expressions of the impersonal All, or Brahma) and of *maya* (by which it is meant that every human deed or condition, whether good or evil, is only an illusion) tend to stultify any conscience a man may have about the evils of society.

Buddhism discusses sin at times; but for the most part "sin" means to the Buddhist any desire. One of "the Ten Sins" according to Buddhism is Love of Life on Earth. It is manifest that if Buddhism despises the earthly life, it will do little to right the evils of society. This has actually been the case.[5] Buddhism tends to minimize mankind's sinful failure.[6]

Confucius and Lao Tse looked on man as simply needing ethical instruction in order to produce a righteous society

---

4. S. H. Kellogg, *A Handbook of Comparative Religion*, p. 46.

5. Cf. Edmund Soper, *The Philosophy of the Christian World Mission*, p. 185.

6. *Cf.* the statement by the Shin sect: "But when a man is very zealous for the propagation of his religion, and offers his whole life, lies, sharp practices, and all, to that end, the whole offering is acceptable and lies and sharp practices, seeing that they become aids to the propagation of the Faith, become parts of an acceptable offering, and are thus accepted." *Ibid.*, p. 184.

on the earth. They did not charge mankind with a corrupt nature. They are cousins to the modern evolutionary thinker who imagines that there is nothing radically wrong with man's moral nature—that he only needs to be given time for the full expression of his ethical longings in order for a just and splendid world society to prevail.

(2) The Biblical Answer

Compare this with the stern denunciation of the Hebrew prophet:

From the sole of the foot even unto the head there is no soundness in it; but wounds, and bruises, and fresh stripes: they have not been closed, neither bound up, neither mollified with oil. (Isaiah 1:6)

The Psalmist wrote:

Jehovah looked down from heaven upon the children of men, to see if there were any that did understand, that did seek after God. They are all gone aside; they are together become filthy; there is none that doeth good, no, not one. (Psalm 14:1-2)

Compare what the New Testament prophet declared of man:

And even as they refused to have God in their knowledge, God gave them up unto a reprobate mind, to do those things which are not fitting; being filled with all unrighteousness, wickedness, covetousness, maliciousness; full of envy, murder, strife, deceit, malignity; whisperers, backbiters, hateful to God, insolent, haughty, boastful, inventors of evil things, disobedient to parents, without understanding, covenant-breakers, without natural affection, unmerciful: who, knowing the ordinance of God, that they that practise such things are worthy of death, not only do the same, but also consent with them that practise them. (Romans 1:28-32)

The modern view of the inherent goodness of man is as old as classic Greek idealism. This taught that the way to the realization of human ethical longings was the progressive development of the natural man, whose reason is directly grounded in the divine reason. Although Kant held to the probability rather than the inevitability of progress, his rational descendants rejected this limitation on human reason. Darwin's speculative conclusions seemed to confirm the idea that man's vices were simply a natural inheritance from the animalistic state and that they would in time be weeded out by the advance of ethical evolution.

The world wars of the last few decades and the continued alarming prevalence of crime[7] have scattered some serious question marks among sayings of the proponents of the inherent goodness of man. But the tendency to excuse himself for his worldwide moral failure is so much a part of the natural man that the statement of Niebuhr still holds:

Modern man has an essentially easy conscience; and nothing gives the diverse and discordant notes of modern culture so much harmony as the unanimous opposition of modern man to Christian conceptions of the sinfulness of man. The idea that man is sinful at the very center of his personality, that is in his will, is universally rejected. It is this rejection which has seemed to make the Christian gospel simply irrelevant to modern man, a fact which is of much more importance than any conviction about its incredibility.[8]

The contrast with the Biblical view could hardly be any sharper.

(1) The Bible teaches that originally man enjoyed unbroken fellowship with God, and nature freely gave her fruit to man; but by disobedience man fell and was driven from the Garden of God and no longer enjoyed full fellowship with him. God sent him out to wrest his living from an accursed ground. But, even so, it was not without hope, for God still provided for them in making clothing for them. Also, he showed them the correct manner of sacrifice for restoration of the broken fellowship.

---

7. In 1953 J. Edgar Hoover reported that there was a major crime committed in the United States every 14.9 seconds.

8. Quoted in Carl F. Henry, *Remaking the Modern Mind*, p. 64.

(2) The Bible teaches that after civilization had progressed for a time, God surveyed it and found it repugnant to himself. The record says that he looked down on the civilization of the world and found it corrupt and violent. Being grieved that he had ever made man, he decided to destroy him; but Noah and his family were saved in an ark.

(3) The Bible states that after the Flood men became so self-willed that God had to scatter them to prevent some great evil which he knew would result if they were allowed to progress as one nation.

(4) God chose Israel as the most promising nation to be his witness of spiritual things to the nations of the world; but Israel eventually became so corrupt that God said of her:

Ah sinful nation, a people laden with iniquity, a seed of evil-doers, children that deal corruptly! they have forsaken Jehovah, they have despised the Holy One of Israel, they are estranged and gone backward. (Isaiah 1:4)

And Jesus foretold that Israel's temple would be desolated, which came to pass under Titus' armies in A.D. 70, at which time the Jews were crucified until there was no more wood to make crosses.

(5) The Bible further teaches that man is so hopelessly defeated in his moral outlook that only the intervention of God can cause justice to prevail in human affairs. It is consistently taught that God has already disapproved natural human society and will ultimately destroy it.

Jesus himself raises a question as to the progressive acceptance of the truth of God in human affairs when he asks (Luke 18:8): "Nevertheless, when the Son of man cometh, shall he find faith on the earth?" He spoke of a time of terrible failure in human society, immediately prior to its final dissolution by God (Matthew 24:29–30).

Paul adds a few strokes to this doleful picture.

For the mystery of lawlessness doth already work: only there is one that restraineth now, until he be taken out of the way, and then shall be revealed the lawless one, whom the Lord

Jesus shall slay with the breath of his mouth, and bring to nought by the manifestation of his coming, even he, whose coming is according to the working of Satan with all power and signs and lying wonders, and with all deceit of unrighteousness for them that perish; because they received not the love of the truth, that they might be saved. (II Thessalonians 2:7–10)

But know this, that in the last days grievous times shall come. For men shall be lovers of self, lovers of money, boastful, haughty, railers, disobedient to parents, unthankful, unholy, without natural affection, implacable, slanderers, without self-control, fierce, no lovers of good, traitors, headstrong, puffed up, lovers of pleasure rather than lovers of God; holding a form of godliness, but having denied the power thereof. . . . Evil men and imposters shall wax worse and worse, deceiving and being deceived. (II Timothy 3:1–5, 13)

Peter affirms that such is the teaching of the whole Bible:

. . . remember the words which were spoken before by the holy prophets, and the commandment of the Lord and Saviour through your apostles: knowing this first, that in the last days mockers shall come with mockery, walking after their own lusts, and saying, Where is the promise of his coming? for, from the day that the fathers fell asleep, all things continue as they were from the beginning of the creation. For this they wilfully forget, that there were heavens from of old, and an earth compacted out of water and amidst water, by the word of God; by which means the world that then was, being overflowed with water, perished: but the heavens that now are and the earth, by the same word have been stored up for fire, being reserved against the day of judgment and destruction of ungodly men. (II Peter 3:2–7)

While some of its passages are to be taken as already fulfilled, the Apocalypse explicitly declares that human society will be dissolved and reorganized by the transcendent intervention of Christ (Revelation 19:11–21:8).

The student with any ability at all for objective generalization will see that the Bible does teach that the continuing and final failure of unaided human society is due to the evil nature of man. We have seen that this denunciation stands in the sharpest contrast with the tendency found everywhere else to excuse man from culpability in this respect. It is human to justify oneself; and those writings so leaning must be looked upon as human. It is unnatural to condemn oneself; and those Biblical writings, produced over a period of many centuries, which pronounce the severest judgment upon man for his sins, must be looked upon as other-than-natural.

CHAPTER IX ❧ *The Bible offers the only satis-factory solution to the problem of sin.*

THE SOLUTION OF THE
SIN PROBLEM

OTHER SCRIPTURES have high moral standards, but no adequate provision for atonement for moral failure, nor does any provide so sublime a moral stimulus for right living as does the Bible. The Bible meets both of these needs in vital harmony.

(1) The Lofty Ethical Teaching of
Other Scriptures

When one is reading the profound moral wisdom of some of the non-Biblical scriptures, he is led to ask why these should not be accepted as on an equal plane with the Bible. Consider, for instance, how ubiquitous is the Golden Rule in all the sacred Scriptures:

BRAHMANISM: "This is the sum of duty: Do naught unto others which would cause you pain if done to you."—*Mahabharata*, 5, 1517

BUDDHISM: "Hurt not others in ways that you yourself would find hurtful."—*Udana-Varga*, 5, 18

CONFUCIANISM: "Is there one maxim which ought to be acted upon throughout one's whole life? Surely it is the maxim of lovingkindness: Do not unto others what you would not have them do unto you."—*Analects*, 15, 23

TAOISM: "Regard your neighbor's gain as your own gain, and your neighbor's loss as your own loss."—*T'ai Shang Kan Ying P'ien*

ZOROASTRIANISM: "That nature alone is good which refrains from doing unto another whatsoever is not good for itself."—*Dadistan-i-dinik*, 94, 5

JUDAISM: "What is hateful to you, do not to your fellowman. That is the entire Law; all the rest is commentary."—*Talmud, Shabbat* 31*a*

CHRISTIANITY: "Therefore all things whatsoever ye would that men should do to you, do ye even so to them: for this is the law and the prophets."—*Matthew* 7:12

ISLAM: "No one of you is a believer until he desires for his brother that which he desires for himself."—*Sunnah*.[1]

Numerous are the bits of moral insight found in even the earliest sacred scriptures, such as these from an ethical fragment of ancient Babylonia:

Whoso takes a bribe, and does not judge righteously, on him thou inflictest punishment. Whoso takes no bribe, but makes intercession for the weak, well-pleasing is this to Shamash, he increaseth his life.[2]

The Code of Hammurabi shows a noble sense of justice in many respects. He proposes to establish justice so that "the strong might not injure the weak, in order to protect the widows and orphans . . . in order to bespeak justice in the land, to settle all disputes."[3] Commendable is Hammurabi's condemnation of slander: "If any one 'point the finger' [slander] at a sister of a god or the wife of any one, and can not prove it, this man shall be taken before the judges and his brow shall be marked."[4]

Fully four thousand years ago Egyptian children were being taught to "be active during the time of thy existence, doing more than is commanded. Do not spoil the time of thy activity; he is a blameworthy person who makes a bad use of his moments."[5] In the fourteenth century B.C. Amenhotep IV in his Hymn to Aton, the Creator, taught his people to worship but one god. He even uses a phrase made familiar

---

1. Lewis Browne, *The World's Great Scriptures*, p. xv.
2. *Ibid.*, p. 8
3. *Ibid.*, pp. 17–18.
4. *Ibid.*, p. 22.
5. *Ibid.*, p. 31.

by Isaiah several centuries later: "beside whom there is no other." [6]

The Hindu scriptures urge us to be generous: "The riches of the generous man never waste away, while he who will not give finds none to comfort him." [7] They give the same high standard for marital fidelity as Christ taught: "Let there be mutual fidelity ending in death alone; this, in short, should be acknowledged as the highest law of duty for man or wife." [8] Krishna, the supreme god of the Hindus, advocates a sacred devotion to duty:

> He who does the task
> Dictated by duty,
> Caring nothing
> For fruit of the action,
> He is a yogi,
> A true monk. [9]

He encourages complete faith in himself:

> Give me your whole heart,
> Love and adore me,
> Worship me always,
> Bow to me only,
> And you shall find me:
> This is my promise
> Who love you dearly.
> Lay down all duties
> In me, your refuge.
> Fear no longer,
> For I will save you
> From sin and from bondage. [10]

Reminiscent of Christ's metaphor of the mote and the beam is the Hindu caution against fault-finding: "The vile

6. *Ibid.*, p. 40. *n.*
7. *Ibid.*, p. 64; from Book X, 121, of the *Rig Veda.*
8. *Ibid.*, p. 96; from Book IX of *The Laws of Manu.*
9. *Ibid.*, p. 108; from "Yoga of Meditation" of the *Bhagavad Gita.*
10. *Ibid.*, p. 118.

are ever prone to detect the faults of others, though they be as small as mustard seeds, and persistently shut their eyes against their own, though they be as large as Vilva fruits." [11]

Buddhism also inculcates a noble ethic. Of the true "brother" it is said:

2. He is incapable of taking what is not given so that it constitutes theft.

3. He is incapable of sexual impurity.

4. He is incapable of deliberately telling lies.

5. He is incapable of laying up treasure for indulgence in worldly pleasure as he used to do in the life of the house.

6. He is incapable of taking a wrong course through partiality.

7. He is incapable of taking a wrong course through hate.

8. He is incapable of taking a wrong course through stupidity.

9. He is incapable of taking a wrong course through fear. [12]

And this is the beginning here for a wise Bhikshu: watchfulness over the senses, contentedness, restraint under the law; keep noble friends whose life is pure, and who are not slothful.

Let him live in charity, let him be perfect in his duties; then in the fulness of delight he will make an end of suffering. . . . [13]

Confucius extols the political, educational, and social virtues. One would indeed be a gentleman and a scholar if he followed the counsels of Confucianism. And what could be a more pertinent principle for our modern world than this:

To obey the will of Heaven is to accept righteousness as the standard. To oppose the will of Heaven is to accept force as the standard. Now what will the standard of righteousness do?

Mo-ti said: He who rules a large state does not attack small states: he who rules a large house does not molest small houses. The strong does not plunder the weak. [14]

---

11. *Ibid.*, p. 126; from *The Garuda Puranam.*
12. *Ibid.*, p. 136; from the *Lakhana Suttanta.*
13. *Ibid.*, p. 186; from "The Bhikshu" of the *Dhammapada.*
14. *Ibid.*, p. 289; from "On the Will of Heaven" of the *Gospel of Mo-ti.*

The scriptures of Taoism, the philosophy of "the Way," approach those of the New Testament when they teach us: ". . . the Sage puts himself last, and finds himself in the foremost place . . ." [15]

The scriptures of Zoroastrianism are exalted in that they teach the ultimate vindication and bliss of the righteous and the ultimate condemnation and misery of the unrighteous.

> O well-disposed believer,
> Hearken not to the followers of the Evil One,
> For these seek to wreck houses,
> Raze villages,
> Despoil clans and provinces;
> They can cause only disaster and death.
> So fight them with all your weapons!
>
> The righteous alone shall be saved
> From destruction and eternal darkness,
> From foul food and the worst curses,
> At the time of the End of Days.
> But ye wicked ones, beware,
> For to these will ye be delivered,
> Because of your evil spirit!
>
> He who serveth Ahura Mazda in mind and deed,
> To him shall be granted the bliss of divine fellowship,
> And fullness of Health,
> Immortality,
> Justice and Power,
> And the Good Disposition. [16]

The Koran inveighs against hypocrisy saying:

O true believers, make not your alms of none effect by reproaching, or mischief, as he who layeth out what he hath to appear unto men to give alms, and believeth not in God and the last day. [17]

---

15. *Ibid.*, p. 298; from the *Tao Teh King*.
16. *Ibid.*, p. 365; from "Yasna XXXI" of the *Gathas*.
17. *Ibid.*, p. 521; from the "Second Surah."

Islam shows a thankful spirit when it says: "If ye attempt to reckon up the favours of God, ye shall not be able to compute their number . . ." [18] The Koran makes every soul responsible for his deeds in a way calculated to cause a man to think before he acts. One is not to fear being punished for the wrongdoing of another.

. . . The fate of every man have we bound about his neck; and we will produce unto him, on the day of resurrection, a book wherein his actions shall be recorded: it shall be offered him open, and the angels shall say unto him, Read thy book; thine own soul will be a sufficient accountant against thee, this day. He who shall be rightly directed, shall be directed to the advantage only of his own soul; and he who shall err shall err only against the same: neither shall any laden soul be charged with the burden of another.[19]

Mohammed prohibits many evils such as pride, fornication, prodigality, economic oppression; there is harsh punishment for the slanderer.

But as to those who accuse women of reputation of whoredom, and produce not four witnesses of the fact, scourge them with fourscore stripes, and receive not their testimony for ever; for such are infamous prevaricators: excepting those who shall afterwards repent, and amend; for unto such will God be gracious and merciful.[20]

(2) The Bible Solution to the Sin Problem Contrasted With Others

After many noble thoughts proposed by the non-Biblical scriptures have been recognized, it is nonetheless incumbent upon the discerning student to note some radical differences between the scriptures of Christianity and those of other religions.

---

18. *Ibid.*, p. 533; from the "Sixteenth Surah."
19. *Ibid.*, p. 533; from the "Seventeenth Surah."
20. *Ibid.*, pp. 537–38; from the "Nineteenth Surah."

One striking difference which the careful student will notice concerns the attitude toward sin and salvation therefrom. In the Bible sin is a transgression of the righteous and beneficent law of God; it is an offense against his morally pure nature; it is a rebellion against his morally perfect will. Because of it man is estranged from God; and man has not the resources to bring about a reconciliation. Because of it man is condemned to death; and he is unable to escape this penalty. Because of his willing participation in sin man is its slave; and he has not the power to break its devilish chains. "But God who is rich in mercy for his great love wherewith he loved us" (Ephesians 2:4), provided a sufficient substitutionary sacrifice to release us from the penalty of sin and a vital moral power to release us from the power of sin, both in the person of his only begotten Son. His infinite death on the cross fulfills the Law's demand that the sinner must die. His limitless love in giving himself for us plants within the redeemed sinner a matchless moral motive of gratitude that is sufficient to insure his subsequent continuance in righteousness. He promises these great blessings to all who will decide to abhor and renounce sin and will cast themselves upon the mercy of God and claim his sacrifice for their sin.

There is a story of a judge whose son was brought before him in court for a serious offense against the law. Knowing the young man's guilt, the judge, in order to uphold the law and to discharge the duty of his office, pronounced the full penalty of the law upon him. Then, laying aside his judicial robes, he stepped down from the bench and paid the son's fine. Then he resumed his place on the bench and declared that the law had been satisfied—the young man was free to go. This is a noble solution to the boy's crime if he makes a proper response to the father's mercy. If he begins to take advantage of it, the father should let him suffer the consequences of his wrongdoing.

The Bible claims that the Son of God, though eternal and infinite spirit, became a human being and lived a normal life among men and allowed himself to be crucified by sinful men as a ransom for many. "God was in Christ reconciling the world unto himself, not reckoning unto them their trespasses . . ." (II Corinthians 5:19). Jesus' presence in the actual historical situation is attested by many witnesses.

When one compares this noble and hope-full concept with the non-Christian answer to sin, he cannot but feel that the difference is as that between a revelation and an inquiry. To be sure, there are flashes of intuition in the various non-Christian Scriptures which are amazingly suggestive of the Christian answer;[21] but these are isolated and have not formed any large part in the religion of the people who follow those respective Scriptures. Taken as a whole, each of the various systems has a decidedly inadequate answer when compared with that of the Bible.

For the Hindu there is no personal God. How can there be sin in the Christian sense against Brahma, the impersonal All of the universe? To orthodox Hinduism concepts of sin and righteousness, good and evil, are alike illusions—*maya.* For the Hindu, "salvation" is not escape from the penalty and power of sin, but escape from the pain incident to believing that life is real—escape by utterly convincing one-

---

21. *Cf.* S. H. Kellogg, *A Handbook of Comparative Religion*, p. 73: "In the primitive Vedic religion of India, there is much which reminds one of the Christian doctrine of the necessity of a Divine atonement to the forgiveness of sin. In the Rig Veda we find expressions such as this: 'Do thou, by means of sacrifice, take away from us all sin.' [Rig Veda x. 133–6.] In the Tandya Maha Brahmana of the Sama Veda it is said of sacrifice: 'Thou art the annulment of sin—of sin!' Not only so, but the doctrine of that early time was that Prajapti, the Lord and Saviour of the universe, gave Himself for men. Thus it is written in the Satapatha Brahmana: 'The Lord of creatures gave Himself for them; for He became their sacrifice.' In the Tait-tiriya Brahmana it is written: 'The sacrifice is the victim; it (the sacrifice) takes the sacrificer to the blessed place.'" *Cf.* the Hindu doctrine of the *Nishkalank Avatar,* or "Sinless Incarnation," who is yet to come. He is supposed to save the good from their oppressors, however, not the sinners from their sins. *Cf.* the Japanese Buddhist sect Shinshu, with its doctrine of salvation by grace through faith alone in Amida Buddha. But this Amida is a figment of the imagination, not an historical person as is Jesus (see Soper, *The Philosophy of the Christian World Mission,* pp. 182–83).

self that the various conditions of life are illusory. For him salvation is to lose one's personal identity by extreme willful concentration upon the abstraction which is reality as opposed to the passions and experiences of human life, in order to be reabsorbed into that Brahma as a drop of sea water falls back into the ocean; whereas for the Christian, salvation is to attain man's true destiny, the highest expression of his personality by the grace of God through union with God in His purpose. There could be no greater ideological difference. Hinduism answers the problem of man's sin by denying its reality—a pitiful answer indeed! The Bible faces sin in all its hideous reality and provides a reasonable and adequate solution for it.

The Buddhistic idea of salvation is similar to the Hindu. It is the attainment of *nirvana*, the cessation of all desire, whether good or evil. A saved Buddhist does not hate (which omission is commendable from a Christian point of view); but neither does he love (which omission is most reprehensible according to the Bible).[22] The souls of the peoples of the East, like those of the West, keep asking, "How can we escape the penalty and power of the ever-present sin?" Buddhism, like Hinduism, out of which it grew, gives a negative solution. For the Hindu, it is, "Deny the reality of conscious existence." For the Buddhist, it is, "Cease to desire and there will be no more evil in the world." Both deny the positive ideal of righteousness which the Bible exalts as the purpose for the creation of man.

It is true that primitive Hinduism, with its *avatars*, and popular Buddhism, with its heavenly *Bodhisat* yet to be born on earth, have a certain resemblance to the sacrificial doctrine of the New Testament; but their "saviors" are only ideas—they have no vestige of historical actuality, whereas Jesus Christ is as well attested historically as any other character of ancient times.

---

22. *E.g.*, I John 4:8: "He that loveth not knoweth not God; for God is love."

Confucius did not concern himself with any doctrine of salvation from sin. He dwelt exclusively on man's relation to man in this present life. Taoism teaches a series of purgatories, which give way to an endless hell if these fail to bring about the man's moral improvement. There is much philosophy about being in the proper state of mind, but no adequate provision for dealing with the problem of sin.

The sacrifices of Mohammedanism are in no way regarded as expiatory. Islam teaches that good deeds will atone for bad ones and bring us acceptance with God. Mohammed had no doctrine of a heaven-provided sacrifice for sin; indeed, according to the Koran, the greatest sin of which a man can be guilty is that of affirming an incarnation.

Thus we see that none of the other great religious Scriptures of the world has provided a satisfactory atonement for sin or so powerful a motive for righteous living as has the Bible. Surely the sublimity of the Biblical doctrine of the solution for sin is a hallmark of its supernatural origin, in view of the universal failure of other age-old scriptures to conceive it.

SUPERNATURAL EFFECTS
ON HUMAN LIFE

THE LAST BUT NOT LEAST of the evidences submitted for the supernatural origin of the Bible is that of the results it produces wherever men believe its words.

(1) The Transformation of Societies

The Bible has transformed the moral characteristics of many peoples.

Alfred Smith, a field missionary for the Young Men's Christian Association, met on a steamer an Anglo-Indian, who, after some conversation, voluntarily gave him a check for one hundred thousand dollars for the furtherance of his work. "Now understand me," said the Englishman, "I am no churchman and don't pretend to be. Then why did I give the money to help along your work? Before you came to India with your missions and clubhouses, life for a business man was not worth living. Now all is changed. I can go away for weeks, knowing that my employees will behave themselves and protect my interests, whereas before my clerks stole from me, my foreman lied to me, my workmen fought and quarreled. And every employer of labour in India will tell you the same story." [1]

James Chalmers, who was martyred in New Guinea, said before a large meeting in London:

I have had twenty-one years' experience among the South Sea Islanders, and for at least nine years of my life I have lived with the savages of New Guinea. I have seen the semi-civilized and the uncivilized; I have lived with the Christian native, and I have

---

1. James G. Lawson, *Best Sermon Pictures*, p. 247.

lived, dined, and slept with the cannibal. But I have never yet
met a single man or woman, or a single people, that your civilization without Christianity has civilized. Wherever there has
been the slightest spark of civilized life in the Southern Seas,
it has been because the gospel has been preached there; and
wherever you find in the Island of New Guinea a friendly people,
or a people that will welcome you, there the missionaries of the
cross have been preaching Christ.[2]

The great difference wrought among savage peoples
when the Bible is accepted is brought out in an anecdote
of the South Sea Islands. Seeing a converted cannibal reading a Bible, a trader said to him, "That book is out of date
in my country." "If it had been out of date here," was the
reply, "you would have been eaten long ago."[3]

No other book has dispelled the great social evils as has
the Bible wherever it has been preached honestly.

Isaac Taylor once attempted a catalogue of the great social evils:
polygamy, legalized prostitution and capricious divorce, bloody
and brutal games, rapacious and offensive wars, death and punishment by torture, infanticide, caste, and slavery. From all lands
where the cross has been set up and the gospel faithfully
preached, these nine gigantic forms of wrong are either retreating or are no more found. A new standard of manhood is also
erected, and new lessons in living are taught. So surely as Christ
becomes Master, so surely do these owls of midnight flee before
the new dawn.[4]

One of the most impressive accounts of the miraculous
effects of the Bible upon a community comes from the pen
of a war correspondent who came in behind the troops in
their bloody victory on Okinawa.

It was an obscure little community of only a few hundred native
Okinawans. Thirty years before, an American missionary on his
way to Japan had stopped here. He hadn't stayed long—just long

---

2. *Ibid.*, p. 249.
3. *Ibid.*, p. 257.
4. *Ibid.*, p. 251.

enough to make a couple of converts, leave them a Bible and then pass on.

One of the converts was Shosei Kina, the other was his brother Mojon. From the time of the missionary's visit, mind you, they had seen no other missionary, had no contact with any other Christian person or group. But in those thirty years Shosei Kina and his brother Mojon had made that Bible come alive. Picking their way through its pages, they had found not only an inspiring Person on whom to pattern a life, but sound precepts on which to base a society.

Aflame with their discovery, they taught the other villagers until every man, woman and child in Shimmabuke was a Christian. Shosei Kina became head man in the village; his brother Mojon, the chief teacher. In Mojon's school the Bible was read daily. To Shosei Kina's village government, its precepts were law. Under the impact of this Book pagan things had fallen away. In their place, during these thirty years, there had developed a Christian democracy at its purest.

Then after thirty years came the American Army, storming across the island. Little Shimmabuke was directly in their path and took some severe shelling. When our advance patrols swept up to the village compound, the GI's, their guns leveled, stopped dead in their tracks as two little old men stepped forth, bowed low and began to speak.

An interpreter explained that the old men were welcoming them as fellow Christians. They remembered that their missionary had come from America. So though these Americans seemed to approach things a little differently than had the missionary, the two men were overjoyed to see them.

The GI's' reaction was typical. Flabbergasted, they sent for the chaplain.

The chaplain came, and with him officers of the Intelligence Service. They toured the village and were astounded at what they saw—the spotlessly clean homes and streets, the poise and gentility of the villagers, the high level of health and happiness, intelligence and prosperity of Shimmabuke. They had seen other villages on Okinawa—villages of unbelievable poverty and ignorance and filth.

Shosei Kina and his brother Mojon observed the Americans' amazement and took it for disappointment. They bowed humbly and said: "We are sorry if we seem a backward people. We have, honored sirs, tried our best to follow the Bible and live like Jesus. Perhaps if you will show us how . . ." *Show them?*

I strolled through Shimmabuke one day with a tough old Army sergeant. As we walked he turned to me and whispered hoarsely, "I can't figure it, fellow—this kind of people coming out of only a Bible and a couple of old guys who wanted to live like Jesus!" Then he added what was to me an infinitely penetrating observation: "Maybe we've been using the wrong kind of weapons to make the world over!" [5]

Think what it would mean . . . if the society of Japan had been developed in the fashion of Shimmabuke! . . . if Russia had taken the spirit of her civilization from the Bible and Jesus! . . . if today the large majority of the nations of the world could be led to build on the spiritual principles of this transforming Book!

(2) The Transformation of Individuals

Because they lend themselves more readily to objective comparison, for the most part only those cases of the reclamation of men who are classed as fallen by *human* standards will be considered, although to the eye of spiritual discernment the change may be just as pronounced in the socially acceptable person who repents and believes.

There can be no doubt that the message of Dwight L. Moody and his associates was a strictly Biblical one. Mr. Ferdinand Schiverea tells of the results of that message in one drunkard's life.

I met a man one night who seemed to be very much troubled, and I soon discovered that he was a drinking man. He had spent from fifty cents to a dollar and a half for drink every day for ten years, and at that time had in his pocket a bottle of medicine to cure the appetite. After talking with him a while he saw that Christ was what he wanted. He knelt down and confessed his

5. Clarence W. Hall, *What I Found At Shimmabuke* (a leaflet published by The American Bible Society).

sins, praying that God would forgive him for breaking his poor old mother's heart, and for grieving his wife, who is now dead, and for neglecting to support his daughter, and promising, if God would forgive him, to be a better man by His help. The next day while at work, his foreman asked him what was the matter with him. He said that he was at the tent the night before and had taken Jesus as his Saviour. I met him about a week afterwards, and he told me it was the happiest week of his whole life, and that he had spent no more money for liquor. The foreman had told him, "If God can save a miserable drunkard like you, he can save me," and promised to come to the tent.[6]

Another of Moody's workers was Merton Smith, who has recorded in his own words the transformation of his life from a state of hungry, drunken, despairing wretchedness to one of joy and life by his acceptance of the message of the cross.[7]

The Pacific Garden Mission of Chicago broadcasts each week over WGN authentic accounts of the transformation of Skid Row men and women who have stumbled into the mission and been led to turn over the government of their lives to the Christ of the New Testament. One such account concerns "Old Harris," a drunken bum who lived among whiskey bottles, cockroaches, greasy playing cards, and dice in a filthy rooming house. One hot summer day he confided to his bartender the reason for his frequent visits to the Pacific Garden Mission. "My room's too blasted hot. Funny smell up there when it get's hot."

"Ever try changing your bed?"

"Sure," he replied. "Twice a year, summer and winter. Summers, I throw off the blankets. Winters, I pull 'em on."

He carried his cynicism to the mission, shouting, "Amen and Amen. Wow!"

Goaded by an unknown impulse after a blasphemous discussion with some mission people, he went into a bookstore and bought a New Testament. In his room he opened it to

---

6. H. M. Wharton, *A Month with Moody in Chicago,* pp. 141–42.
7. *Ibid.,* pp. 155 ff.

the place where it says: "Thou fool, this night thy soul shall be required of thee."

He threw the book down, but could not escape the thrust of the words. After much groping in the dimly lighted room, he retrieved the book and, not knowing how to find the verse again, started reading from the first page until he came to it. That night he went to the mission, knelt down with Mother Clarke and prayed.

"I'm fixing to pray. I'm fixing to ask God to clean me up. Lord? You hear me, can You? Here I am, like I promised. I ain't got no good in me to give You. It's all black and sinful and dirty. I'm sorry about all the times I cussed You, God. For Jesus' sake."

Later on, on his way to his room, Harris shook his fist at the saloons as he went by them. He mounted the stairs in a hurry, went to his room. With one sweep, he ripped the pictures off the wall. "Don't belong here now, I'm a Christian." He dumped his dice, his wallets, empty whiskey bottles into one of the boxes stacked in the corner and shoved it out into the hall. "You're done, too," he said.

"Want a bucket of hot water," he told his landlady. After he had scrubbed down the walls and woodwork, he scrubbed the ceiling, swept up his cigar butts, scrubbed the floor, and foraged for clean sheets. "Everythin's gotta be clean," he told his cronies. "I'm clean. I was washed in the blood of the Lamb, my Saviour, Jesus Christ." Then he laid his New Testament on the table beside the bed.[8]

Many such case histories of the transforming power of the Bible message are in the Pacific Garden Mission files.

Mr. Paul J. Loizeaux has related his conversations with the convict, Daniel Mann, before the latter was executed for killing a penitentiary guard. After a period of spiritual struggle, the prisoner sincerelly put his faith in the Christ of the New Testament. Through the weeks that followed until the time of his death his face uniformly displayed the joyful change which had come over him. He did not use his con-

---

8. From *Unshackled,* by Eugenia Price and Faith Coxe Bailey, pp. 13 ff.

version as a plea for amelioration of his sentence, but as a means of witness to the other prisoners and the guards.

At one time, as he lay resting on the bench, his coat rolled up under his head for a pillow, his happiness became so intense that he said to me, "I do not believe I can live till morning." His eyes closed, his hands lifted toward heaven, he only gave signs of life by repeating in a low voice, "Lord Jesus, one with Thee! I long for Thee, Lord Jesus!" After this, he slept a little while. When he awoke, he asked me what time it was. "It is just three o'clock," I said.

"Five hours more, my blessed Jesus, and I shall be with Thee," he said. "Oh, how sweet that is! I never knew what real unbroken, unclouded happiness was even until last Saturday, when I saw Christ in heaven as my righteousness." [9]

On the morning of his execution he called the night guard and said:

"Oh, Mr. R., I love you: I do love you much, and I wish I could see you resting in Christ before I die!"

"I have determined now to try to be a Christian," answered the guard.

"Oh, no, that will not do! that will not do!" he replied. "God wants none of *your* determination. It is His Son, eternal life, a finished redemption, *He* offers you. Will you not have it? Look at me. Three hours more and I shall hang, and yet I am the happiest man living. What do you think of that? Is there not reality in Christ? Is it not a reality worth having?" [10]

A missionary-colporteur of Brazil bears testimony to the miraculous work of a Bible on the life of another criminal, Pedro Feliz, who as a youth had been an accomplice in the robbery and murder of an old woman. Having served fifteen of his thirty-year sentence, he got hold of a Bible, taught himself to read it, and believed its message. Thereafter, in the unbelievable filth and stench of a Brazilian prison, he

---

9. P. J. Loizeaux, *The Lord's Dealings with the Convict Daniel Mann,* pp. 57–58.

10. *Ibid.,* p. 60.

became known as "the Happy Convict." From his meager income as the prison cobbler he saved money for support of the work of Bible distribution. Surely nothing short of a supernatural book could work so great a wonder on a man who faced fifteen more years of such an outwardly dreary existence.[11]

As a seminary student the author remembers hearing Dr. Harold Ironsides relate an incident in which a prominent atheist on the west coast publicly challenged him to a debate on the validity of Christianity. Dr. Ironsides replied by choosing the terms of the contest as follows. At the appointed time he would bring twenty persons who had been drunkards, prostitutes, or otherwise living in moral degradation, who would testify that trusting in the message of the Bible had brought about their reclamation. His opponent was to bring twenty such persons who would testify that following the atheist's doctrine had restored them to decent and useful living. The man looked at the preacher a moment and then left the platform with a curious wave-off of his hands in the manner of a theatrical exit. The atheist knew that his gospel of human self-sufficiency could not transform fallen men as does the Gospel of Christ.

The writer personally knows of numbers of men who would no doubt today still be living in drunken debauchery had they not trusted in the message of the Bible. They themselves bear witness that it is the message of the New Testament that has remade them. This miraculous power of the Bible to transform human life is proof of its divine origin.

---

11. F. C. Glass, *Adventures with the Bible in Brazil,* pp. 66 ff.

CONCLUSION

AT THE BEGINNING, we noticed that the authority of the Bible is being rejected by many Christians in favor of the authority of personal experience. It is the position of this study that such an attitude is productive of many ills for the cause of Christ. Our personal experience with God is a result of our acceptance of the authority of his instructions. The word of God is not determined by our personal experience; but our personal experience is determined by the word of God. Personal experience is not the authority in dealing with God's law any more than it is the authority in dealing with man's law. Of course, we have to exercise our reason in order to grasp the import of the law; still, our personal judgment is not the standard, but the laws as written on the statute books. Evangelical Christians need to understand that if personal experience is the authority in religion, then liberal Christians are right in insisting that Buddhists, Hindus, Moslems, and other non-Christians have just as much foundation for their religion as we do for ours.

J. K. van Baalen has written a book entitled *Chaos of Cults*, the idea being that there is a veritable confusion of religious beliefs in the world today. The religions and sects which differ radically from the evangelical tradition of Christianity are those which have forsaken or never had the acceptance-of-the-Bible as their fundamental doctrine. Animism, Hinduism, Buddhism, Taoism, Confucianism, and Islam, of course, have never accepted the authority of the Bible. Judaism long ago began to give most of its attention to the Rabbinical traditions, which often in spirit contradicted the Scriptures. Similarly, ecclesiasticism early exalted its ecclesiastical dicta over that of the word of God. Christian sects which cannot have fellowship with evangelical

Christianity are those which have exalted some other authority over that of the Bible. Liberal Christianity is characterized chiefly by liberty from the authority of God's word. Indeed, if man is left to his own subjective notions about the will of Heaven, we will have a veritable hodgepodge of religious ideas. On the other hand, because God has given us an objective standard, there are multiplied millions of people around the world who form a common fellowship, united around the acceptance of the commands of God as given in the Bible. In spite of minor differences of interpretations of God's word, these agree on the primary themes of the Bible: the sinful nature of man; his estrangement from God; eternal death for sin; the deity of Jesus; his virgin birth; his blood atonement for sin; salvation by grace through faith; Christ's bodily resurrection; and his future bodily return. This is the *kerugma*—the fundamental message of original Christianity—from which there have been many deviations since New Testament times. In this *kerugma* we find the true homogeneity of Christianity of all times and of all places. For the most part this common faith today cuts across denominational lines. There are in almost all Christian denominations individuals who accept the authority of the Bible, sometimes in spite of the official teachings of their communions. There are those who play up the differences among those who take the Bible as their standard; but to the eye of faith there stands a mighty host of people who alike have found God's will and are doing it. Beneath the apparent differences there lies an inner spiritual oneness that is not found elsewhere. This unity comes from the recognition of a Book that bears all the marks of supernatural origin upon its pages.

BIBLIOGRAPHY

ARCHAEOLOGY

Adams, J. M., *Biblical Backgrounds.* 1934.
Ceram, C. W., *Gods, Graves and Scholars.* 1952.
Muir, J. C., *The Spade and the Scriptures.* 1940.
Rimmer, Harry, *Dead Men Tell Tales.* Fifth Edition, 1943.
Unger, Merrill, *Archaeology and the Old Testament.* Second edition, 1954.

AUTHORITY OF THE BIBLE

Chirgwin, A. M., *The Bible in World Evangelism.* 1954.
DeVries, John, *Beyond the Atom.* Second edition, 1950.
Engelder, T. H., *The Scripture Cannot Be Broken.* 1944.
Henry, Carl F., *Remaking the Modern Mind.* 1946.
Ramm, Bernard, *The Christian View of Science and Scripture.* 1955.
Rimmer, Harry, *The Harmony of Science and Scripture.* 1940.
Smith, Wilbur M., *Therefore, Stand.* 1950.

COMMENTARY

Burton, Ernest, *The Epistle to the Galatians.* 1948.
Clarke, W. K. L., *Concise Bible Commentary.* 1953.
Delitzch, Franz, *Isaiah.* Fourth edition; 1910.
Elliott, Charles J., editor, *The Handy Bible Commentary.* N.d.
Halley, Henry H., *Pocket Bible Handbook.* Nineteenth edition, 1951.
Redpath, H. A., *Ezekiel.* 1907.

COMPARATIVE RELIGION

Browne, Lewis, *The World's Great Scriptures.* 1946.
Kellogg, S. H., *A Handbook of Comparative Religion.* 1951.

Soper, Edmund D., *The Philosophy of the Christian World Mission*. 1943.
——, *The Religions of Mankind*. 1938.

CRITICAL STUDY

Allis, Oswald T., *The Five Books of Moses*. Second edition, 1949.
——, *The Unity of Isaiah*. 1950.
Dana, H. E., *The Ephesian Tradition*. 1940.
Francisco, C. T., *The Authorship and Unity of Isaiah 40–66*. Th.D. thesis, Southern Baptist Theological Seminary. 1944.
Goodspeed, Edgar J., *The Story of the Old Testament*. 1940.
Pfeiffer, R. H., *Introduction to the Old Testament*. 1941.
Smith, G. A., *The Book of Isaiah*. Two volumes, 1927.

EVOLUTION

Dawson, W. Bell, *Opinions of Scientists on Evolution*. Pamphlet N.d.
Evolution, an anonymous booklet published by International Christian Crusade (366 Bay St., Toronto, Canada). Eleventh Edition, revised, 1951.
Innes, T. Christie, *Darwinism: Faith or Science?* N.d.
Watts, Newman, *This Is Serious!* Pamphlet. N.d.

GRAMMAR

Brown, F., Driver, and Briggs, *A Hebrew and English Lexicon*. 1907.
Robertson, A. T., *A New Short Grammar of the Greek New Testament*. 1933.

HISTORY

Daniel-Rops, *Sacred History*. 1949.
King, L. W., *History of Babylon*. 1915.
Toynbee, Arnold, *A Study of History*. Abridgment by D. C. Somervell. 1947.
Wells, H. G., *The Outline of History*. 1920.
Whiston, William, *The Life and Works of Flavius Josephus*. N.d.

Bibliography

LIBERAL ATTITUDE TOWARD INSPIRATION

Bowie, Walter Russell, *The Bible Story for Boys and Girls, Old Testament.* 1952.

Eakin, Frank and Mildred M., *Let's Think About Our Religion.* 1944.

Ferris, Theodore P., *This Created World.* 1944.

Fosdick, H. E., *A Guide to Understanding the Bible.* 1938.

——, *The Modern Use of the Bible.* 1942.

MISCELLANEOUS

Encyclopedia Britannica, The. Eleventh edition, 1910.

Hall, Clarence W., *What I Found at Shimmabuke,* a leaflet published by The American Bible Society. N.d.

Knight, W. B., *Three Thousand Illustrations for Christian Service.* 1940.

Lawson, James G., *Best Sermon Pictures.* N.d.

Loizeaux, P. J., *The Lord's Dealings With the Convict Daniel Mann.* 1911.

Price, Eugenia, and F. C. Bailey, *Unshackled.* Second edition, 1953.

Roberts, W. H., *The Problem of Choice.* 1941.

Spreading the Light, a leaflet published by The American Bible Society.

Webster's Collegiate Dictionary. Fifth edition, 1944.

Wharton, H. M., *A Month With Moody in Chicago.* 1894.

MISSIONS

Glass, F. C., *Adventures With the Bible in Brazil.* 1943.

Lambdin, Ina S., *Trail-Makers in Other Lands.* 1929.

MYTHOLOGY

Bulfinch, Thomas, *Bulfinch's Mythology,* N.d.

De Meiss-Teuffen, Hans, with Victor Rosen, *Wanderlust.* 1953.

Howells, William, *Back of History.* 1954.

Ingstadt, Helge, *Nunamiut.* 1951.

NATURAL SCIENCE

Fenton, Carroll L., *Our Amazing Earth*. 1941.

PHILOSOPHY

Berman, Louis, *Behind the Universe*. 1943.
Durant, Will, *The Story of Philosophy*. 1926; revised 1933.

TEXTUAL CRITICISM

Dupont-Sommer, *The Dead Sea Scrolls*. 1952.
Robertson, A. T., *An Introduction to the Textual Criticism of the New Testament*. 1925.

INDEX